The Fifth French Republic

The Fifth French Republic offers an introduction to modern French politics and history which focuses on the careers and personalities of the five men elected to the Presidency since the establishment of the regime in 1958: Charles de Gaulle, Georges Pompidou, Valéry Giscard d'Estaing, François Mitterrand and Jacques Chirac.

The book describes how the Fifth French Republic came into existence, and discusses the way in which it differs from previous attempts to establish a viable democratic régime in France. It compares the version of democracy represented by the Fifth French Republic with the longer established constitutional practices in the English-speaking democracies, and pays particular attention to the role of the French civil service. Other topics treated include:

- decolonisation, and de Gaulle's solution to the Algerian problem
- French attitudes to the European Union
- the behaviour of France during the Cold War
- the experiment in socialism under François Mitterrand
- attempts at decentralisation and at reducing the role of the state
- anti-Americanism in France
- the problems of immigration and the rise of the National Front

Philip Thody is Emeritus Professor at Leeds University and the author of *The Conservative Imagination, French Caesarism from Napoleon I to Charles de Gaulle* and *An Historical Introduction to the European Union*.

The Fifth French Republic

Presidents, politics and
personalities

Philip Thody

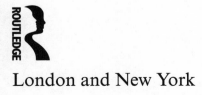

London and New York

First published 1998
by Routledge
11 New Fetter Lane, London EC4P 4EE

Simultaneously published in the USA and Canada
by Routledge
29 West 35th Street, New York, NY 10001

©1998 Philip Thody

Typeset in Bembo by Routledge
Printed and bound in Great Britain by Redwood Books, Trowbridge,
Wiltshire

British Library Cataloguing in Publication Data
A catalogue record for this book is available from the British Library

Library of Congress Cataloging-in-Publication Data
has been applied for

ISBN 0–415–18754–0 (pbk)
ISBN 0–415–18753–2 (hbk)

Geography is about maps. History is about chaps.

Pre-feminist and pre-postmodernist dictum

Contents

Acknowledgements

As in previous books, I am most grateful to my friend and colleague, Howard Evans, for all his help and advice. All mistakes are naturally my own.

Glossary

Institutions mentioned in the text include:

La Confédération Générale du Travail (CGT) a trade-union grouping sympathetic to the French Communist Party.

Le Conseil d'État the highest court in France for administrative law, and the body which the government must consult before submitting a bill (projet de loi) to Parliament and a member of parliament before presenting Parliament with a proposition de loi (Private Member's Bill).

Corps de l'Éducation Nationale All teachers in the state sector of education in France are civil servants. As the Note on the French civil service in Appendix C explains, every civil servant in France belongs to a corps, which provides the basis for her or his official status.

La Cour des Comptes the court of law responsible for checking the use of all public money in France.

L'École Nationale d'Administration (ÉNA) the post-graduate school responsible for the training of senior civil servants. It fulfils a different role, and enjoys higher prestige, than the Civil Service College in Great Britain.

L'École Normale Supérieure one of the Grandes Écoles which differ from French universities by having a competitive entry system (concours), and providing education for a specific career, in this case as teachers in secondary schools and universities.

Grands Corps de l'État a generic term used to describe Le Conseil d'État and La Cour des Comptes (see above) and l'Inspection des Finances (see below). Their members are normally recruited from the ÉNA, and constitute the élite of the French civil service. They do not normally accept the view of the members of the Corps Diplomatique that they too belong to a Grand Corps.

Inspection des Finances the smallest of the Grands Corps de l'État. It is responsible both for checking the accounts of other ministries and for offering advice as to the most economically efficient way of implementing government policy.

Mouvement Républicain Populaire (MRP) a moderately left-wing Catholic party, formed as a result of the participation of Roman Catholics in the resistance movement, and strongly in favour of a united Europe.

Rassemblement du Peuple Français (RPF) a political grouping formed by Charles de Gaulle on April 8, 1947 in order to enable him to come back to power and change the constitution of the Fourth Republic. It did not succeed, and de Gaulle dissolved it in June 1953. After his return to power in 1958, a political party was formed to support him under the name of L'Union pour la Nouvelle République (UNR). In November 1967, this became L'Union des démocrates pour la Ve République (U.D. Ve Rép.), and in June 1968, L'Union pour la Défense de la République (UDR). In 1971, this became L'Union des Démocrates pour la République.

On December 6, 1976, after resigning as prime minister, Jacques Chirac formed his own party, Le Rassemblement pour la République (RPR). On January 1, 1978, Chirac's opponents formed the right-wing grouping which has tended to support Giscard d'Estaing, L'Union pour la Démocratie Française (UDR).

Note: In accordance with modern publishing practice, and with the recommendation in Judith Butcher's *The Cambridge Handbook for Copy-Editing for Authors, Editors and Publishers* that roman type should be used for 'proper names such as institutions and streets', these terms are not italicised.

Introduction

Technically, seven men have held office as president of the Fifth French Republic: René Coty, Charles de Gaulle, Alain Poher, Georges Pompidou, Valéry Giscard d'Estaing, François Mitterrand and Jacques Chirac. This book deals only with the five to have been elected under the Constitution adopted by referendum on September 28, 1958. They are Charles de Gaulle, Georges Pompidou, Valéry Giscard d'Estaing, François Mitterrand and Jacques Chirac.

René Coty had been elected president of the Fourth Republic on December 23, 1953. He remained in office after the referendum of September 28, 1958 had approved the proposed Constitution of the Fifth Republic, which he promulgated on October 4. Charles de Gaulle was elected president on December 21, 1958, and formally took over from René Coty on January 8, 1959.

On April 27, 1969 it was announced that de Gaulle's proposals on regionalisation and the reform of the Senate had been rejected by referendum. De Gaulle immediately resigned, and did not therefore complete the second seven-year mandate to which he had been elected on December 19, 1965. The president of the Senate, Alain Poher, acted in accordance with Article 7 of the Constitution of 1958 and took over the role of president on a temporary basis. He stood as a candidate in the presidential election of June 1 and June 15, 1969, but was defeated in the second round. On June 20, he handed over the presidency to Georges Pompidou.

On April 2, 1974, Pompidou died in office. Unlike the Constitution of the United States of America, the Constitution of the Fifth French Republic has no office of vice-president, one of whose responsibilities it is to take over in the event of the president's death, and remain in office until the next scheduled presidential election takes place. Alain Poher therefore once again became president on a temporary basis, but was not a candidate in the presidential election of May 5 and May 12,

1974, made necessary by Pompidou's death. On May 27, 1974, he handed over the presidency to Valéry Giscard d'Estaing, who on May 19 had defeated François Mitterrand in the second round of the presidential election.

On May 8, 1981, Giscard d'Estaing failed to win a second term against the socialist candidate, François Mitterrand. Mitterrand then became the fourth president of the Fifth Republic to be elected under the Constitution of 1958, and the first socialist to hold the office. On May 8, 1988, François Mitterrand succeeded in winning a second term, but did not stand for re-election on completing his second seven-year period in 1995. On May 7, 1995, the right-wing Gaullist candidate Jacques Chirac defeated the socialist Lionel Jospin to become the fifth president of the Fifth French Republic to be elected under the 1958 Constitution.

Each of the five men so far to have been elected to the office of president of the Fifth Republic began his working life as a salaried servant of the state. Each performed honourably on the field of battle. Each tended to appoint former civil servants to the office of prime minister. Each was married and had children, and each had ambitions, more successfully achieved in some cases than in others, to be a writer as well as a politician. De Gaulle's *Mémoires* show him to have been no less a master of French prose than Winston Churchill was of the English language. Georges Pompidou published an anthology of French poetry as well as a very readable volume of reminiscences.

Valéry Giscard d'Estaing said that he would rather have been Flaubert or Maupassant than a practising politician, and went so far as to publish a novel. Mitterrand was a prolific author of philosophical meditations as well as of political pamphlets. When elected, in 1981, he chose to have the official photograph taken of him holding a book. It was, he wished to suggest, for his writings that wished primarily to be remembered, rather than for his activity as a politician. Jacques Chirac has so far published five books expressing his political beliefs.[1]

Each of the five presidents of the Fifth Republic was brought up as a member of the Roman Catholic Church. With the exception of François Mitterrand, each remained a practising Catholic, and Mitterrand himself chose to have a religious funeral. Historically, French republicanism has always placed great emphasis on the secular nature of the state. Religious belief nevertheless remains a major sign of social and political respectability. As the first president of the Fourth Republic, Vincent Auriol commented in his diary for 1953, as the time approached for the election of his successor. 'Je ne sais pas qui sera président de la République. Mais ce que je sais, c'est qu'il ira à la messe' (I don't know who will be President of the Republic. But what I do know is that he will go to Mass).[2]

Each of the five presidents made a notable contribution to the physical appearance of Paris. In the 1960s, Charles de Gaulle encouraged his minister of culture, the novelist and art historian André Malraux, to undertake the cleaning of the major buildings of the capital by the newly invented technique of *ravalement*, or sand-blasting. Georges Pompidou gave new life to a neglected part of the right bank by building the Centre Pompidou in the Place Beaubourg. Valéry Giscard d'Estaing inspired the transformation of former Gare d'Orsay, on the left bank of the Seine, into the Musée du XIXe siècle. François Mitterrand was responsible for Le Grand Louvre, L'Arche de la Défense, l'Opéra Bastille, and La Très Grande Bibliothèque. From 1976 onwards, Jacques Chirac was mayor of Paris, and made it one of the cleanest cities in the Western world. Without his co-operation, none of Giscard d'Estaing's or Mitterrand's projects could have gone ahead.

De Gaulle had already had an impressive if controversial political career before being elected president. Both François Mitterrand and Jacques Chirac succeeded only on their third attempt, a fact which led to the comment in *Le Monde* for April 25, 1997 that the French liked to see their presidents well covered with the scars of electoral battle before they entrusted them with the cares of the supreme office. This explains the attention given in each chapter of this book to what the president whose career it describes did before being elected.

1 Charles de Gaulle

The founding father

Generalities

Two crises gave Charles de Gaulle the opportunity of achieving the ambition which he described in the opening pages of the first volume of his *Mémoires de Guerre*, *L'Appel*, when he wrote of the vision of France which had inspired his early years:

> Enfin, je ne doutais pas que l'intérêt de la vie consistait à lui rendre quelque service signalé, et que j'en aurais l'occasion. (Finally, I had no doubt that life's interest lay in rendering my country some outstanding service, and that I would have the chance to do so).

The first crisis arose in the early summer of 1940, when the armies of the Third Reich conquered France. The second became acute in May 1958, when a group of Algerian Europeans, supported by the French army, seized power in Algiers and called upon de Gaulle to assume power. The ability which he showed in solving the Algerian problem derived directly from the reputation he had won between 1940 and 1944.

It could certainly be argued, especially from the standpoint of the 1990s, that what de Gaulle did between 1940 and 1944 was more important for the myth which it created than for any long-term need which he satisfied. No other Western European country had a de Gaulle to assume the leadership of its destiny during the second world war. But all the countries of Western Europe were restored, after they had been liberated by the armies of the English-speaking democracies, to the same position in which they could order their affairs as they chose.

France alone, however, found itself in the kind of situation created in 1958 by the Algerian war, and where it could solve a major political problem only by calling on a charismatic military leader. France alone, among the countries of Western Europe freed from German occupation after 1944, went through a crisis which led to a change of constitution and a different way of making democracy work. France alone both had and needed a de Gaulle.

It is, among the countries of Western Europe, a peculiarity of French political life to have recourse to a military man at a moment of real or alleged national crisis. Neither Hitler nor Mussolini was a professional soldier, and although General Franco ruled Spain as a dictator between 1939 and 1975, it was after a bloody civil war, not after a relatively short crisis solved by the arrival of an apparently providential military leader. French military men, in contrast, take power after *coups d'état* which are brief and relatively bloodless. They then govern through civilian administrators, and their main achievements are in domestic rather than in foreign policy.[1]

De Gaulle remained faithful to this tradition by the kind of men he appointed to serve under him, and it was in many ways his greatest triumph to have succeeded in imposing his solution to the Algerian problem on a body of professional soldiers who wanted to keep Algeria French. But in his ability, on two occasions, to use his prestige as a military leader to take charge in a crisis, and to move from a career in which he served the state as one of its salaried officials to one where he took charge of its destinies, he expresses an aspect of French political behaviour with which there is no parallel in the political culture of any other country.

1890–1940

On September 27, 1909, de Gaulle entered the cavalry school at Saint-Cyr, and signed on for an initial engagement of four years. He remained a professional soldier after the first world war, and had spent forty years in the army when he entered politics by leaving for London and making the broadcast on June 18, 1940, in which he declared that France had lost a battle but had not lost the war.

He served with distinction in the first world war. He was awarded the Croix de Guerre, and was three times wounded in action. After the armistice, he served with the Polish army fighting on the side of the White Russians during the civil war which followed the Bolshevik revolution of October 1917. On February 1, 1922, he came back to France and taught history at Saint-Cyr. In the *concours de sortie* (competitive leaving examination), at Saint-Cyr in 1911, he had come 13 out of 211, an improvement on his performance in the *concours d'entrée* in 1909, where he came 94th.

Considerable importance is attached in France to the place one obtains in the various *concours* which punctuate any respectable career in the public service. This place does not, however, always have a predictive value. Jean Bichelonne, *sorti major* (who came top) at the l'École Polytechnique in 1927, with the highest marks ever awarded, collaborated enthusiastically with the Vichy régime of 1940–4. He had proved to himself statistically that Germany was bound to win the second world war.[2]

In May 1922, de Gaulle was successful in the *concours d'entrée* at the École de Guerre (Staff College), where he entered 33rd out of 129, but came out lower at 52. He was beginning to show the reluctance to accept other people's opinions which was to become such a marked feature of his personality, and Marshal Pétain had to intervene personally in order to ensure that he received the overall *mention bien* instead of the *mention passable* that the examiners were preparing to give him.

The lesson which de Gaulle's senior officers had drawn from the first world war was that defence had become more important than attack, and was likely to remain so. It was a view which led to the decision, on December 29, 1929, to build the Maginot line along the frontier between France and Germany. In any future war, it was argued, the Germans would not come either through Belgium or the Ardennes, but would exhaust themselves by attacking this impregnable line of fortifications, and go home in despair. Or, since they could see that they could never successfully invade France, they would simply not start another war.

De Gaulle had a different vision. For him, as he argued in his major pre-war work, *Vers l'armée de métier*, published in May 1934, the French High Command had drawn the wrong lesson from the failure of make use of the breakthrough achieved by the first use of tanks at Cambrai by the British on November 20, 1917. Because soldiers on foot had not been able to keep up with the speed of their advance, the doctrine developed that tanks should be allowed to advance only at the speed of the infantry. They were, therefore, to be used only in support, and not as a mobile striking force in their own right.

De Gaulle argued the exact opposite, and did so for political as well as military reasons. There was, he maintained, no point in France signing alliances with relatively small countries in Eastern Europe, as she had done with Poland, Czechoslovakia and Rumania in the early 1920s, since there was nothing she could do to help them if they were attacked. The decision to spend all the money available for defence on

De Gaulle Found Best solution

building the Maginot line was a sign to Germany that she had a free hand in Eastern Europe. Whatever she did, France would not intervene, because she had denied herself the means of doing so. If, on the other hand, France were to build a mobile striking force, she would not only be able to defend herself in any future war of movement. By her ability to use this force to attack Essen, Dusseldorf or Cologne, she could deter Germany from any aggressive action anywhere in Europe.

It was, in an early form, a version of the concept of the deterrent which President Eisenhower was to formulate more clearly in the confrontation with China over the islands of Quemoy and Matsu in 1954 when he spoke of the United States being able to carry out a policy of 'massive retaliation at a time and place of our own choosing'. De Gaulle's ideas might even, had they been adopted by Great Britain as well as France, have prevented the second world war from taking place, in the same way as the threat of the nuclear deterrent kept the peace during the Cold War between 1945 and 1989. But de Gaulle failed in his first attempt to play a political role, and did so both because of the nature of the society which he was trying to influence and through the defects of his own character.

Like the Great Britain of the 1920s and 1930s, France was a country which simply wanted to be left alone. She had had over 1,300,000 men killed between 1914 and 1918, and almost a million seriously wounded. She had one of the lowest birthrates in Western Europe. She still had the illusion of having won the first world war, and had not had the consequences of the war forced home to her, as Germany had, by having had part of her territory occupied, her pre-war régime destroyed, her economy ruined and her currency made worthless by the financial crisis of 1923. She had, unlike Germany, no longing for revenge.

The Third Republic also had the disadvantage, especially in de Gaulle's eyes, of being what is known as a *régime d'assemblée*. The president was a figurehead, and not always an impressive one at that. There were so many political parties that every government was a coalition. The principal task of the Président du Conseil des Ministres (Chairman of the Council of Ministers; the term Premier Ministre was not introduced until 1958) was to try to hold the coalition together, a situation which de Gaulle illustrated by the account which he gave in *L'Appel*, the first volume of his *Mémoires de Guerre*, of the interview which he had with Léon Blum on October 14, 1936.

Blum had recently become Président du Conseil in the Popular Front government brought to power by the victory of the left in the elections of April 26 and May 3, and was more prepared than he had been in the past to listen to de Gaulle's arguments in favour of a mobile striking force. But during their conversation the telephone rang ten times, on each occasion presenting Blum with some urgent question of parliamentary tactics. There was no way, de Gaulle realised, that the head of a government in circumstances such as these would ever be able to do anything positive. When he eventually came to power, in 1958, nobody was allowed to telephone him. He would, occasionally, ring them, but would take no calls. There was also a notice outside his bedroom door which bore the inscription: 'A déranger uniquement en cas de guerre mondiale' (To be disturbed only in the event of a world war).

The Third Republic was not a perfect régime. Its collapse in 1940 exposed the French people to four years of occupation by the Germans, and to the humiliation of being the only country whose official rulers advocated a policy of collaboration with Nazi Germany. But there is more to be said is its favour than de Gaulle allows. There is also more to criticise in his own conduct than is ever suggested by the hypnotic power which the prose of the *Mémoires de Guerre* exercises over its readers.

The laws of 1881 and 1882, introduced by Jules Ferry (1832–93), and creating l'École nationale, gratuite, obligatoire et laïque, in many ways epitomise what the Third Republic did best. They changed France from a country in which fewer than 10 per cent of the population could read and write to one where it was highly abnormal to be illiterate. By insisting on the need to exclude the teaching of formal religious belief, they laid the foundations for a modern democratic society which neither the Roman Catholic Church nor the French monarchist movement would otherwise ever have accepted.

In his eulogy for one of the most successful politicians not to have become president of the Republic, Pierre Mendès France pointed out that Jules Ferry did more than inspire the laws of 1881 and 1882 which taught the French people to read and write. It was also to his impulsion that the French owed four other major pieces of progressive legislation: the law of 1884 giving legal existence to trade unions; the loi Naquet of 1885 authorising divorce; the central role of the mayor in their system of local government; and the law of July 29, 1881 establishing the freedom of the press, nowadays known to most people only through the frequency of its interdict inscribed on the walls of French towns in the form 'Défense d'afficher selon la loi du 29 juillet 1881'.[3] It gave the jury, and not the state-appointed judge, the authority to decide cases of alleged libel. Like the other achievements of the Third Republic, such as the winning of the 1914–18 war, or the institution by the Popular Front of 1936 of paid holidays for all workers, it is another indication of how well the Third Republic could serve its citizens, even without the strong presidency which de Gaulle regarded as essential for the successful survival of any régime in France.

De Gaulle's failure to persuade the authorities to create the mobile striking force which might have saved France in 1940 was also due to his own personality. When he came to England in June 1940, not a single man who had served under his orders came to join him. Churchill's comment that the heaviest cross he had to bear during the second world war was the Cross of Lorraine would also have drawn nods of approval from some of de Gaulle's brother officers. In November 1929, they are said to have threatened to resign en masse if de Gaulle was appointed to a permanent post as a lecturer at the École de Guerre. He was therefore posted to Syria, before being brought back to Paris in 1931 and appointed to the Secrétariat général de la Défense nationale.[4]

It was at almost exactly the same time that Admiral Darlan (1881–1943) was, by contrast, achieving great success in obtaining the credits necessary to realise his ambition of making the French navy the fourth largest in the world, immediately after those of Great Britain, Germany and the United States of America. It is an instructive example of what a sailor with an accommodating personality, and who is prepared to spend his time in the corridors of power rather than on the quarterdeck, can do for his service. Although de Gaulle had written, as early as 1932, that 'la perfection évangélique ne mène point à l'empire. L'homme d'action ne se conçoit pas sans une forte dose d'égoïsme, d'orgueil, de dureté, de ruse' (Evangelical perfection offers no path to empire. The man of action is inconceivable without a strong dose of egotism, pride, harshness and cunning),[5] he was able to put this precept into practice only much later in his career.

One of the serious errors of tactics which de Gaulle had made in 1934 was to give his book the title *Vers l'armée de métier* (Towards a professional army). The *levée en masse* of August 23, 1793 had made France the first country in the modern world to require all its male citizens between 18 and 35 to do military service. But ever since the *coups d'état* of 1799, 1851 and 1852 by which Napoleon Bonaparte and his nephew Louis-Napoleon had seized power, the republican tradition had insisted on the desirability of a citizen army. Only by having all male citizens under arms, it was thought, could the Republic defend itself against the danger of another dictator using the army as the modern equivalent of the Praetorian guard.

If de Gaulle had adopted a French equivalent of the title under which his book appeared in English, *Towards the Army of the Future*, he would have encountered less resistance among *les vrais républicains*. But he was never the most tactful of men, and it was for political considerations of this kind that the authorities of the Third Republic did not do as the Germans did and group all its most modern weaponry under the command of one man. Had it done so, and had the High Command also realised, as Hitler did, how powerful the combination between dive bombers and tanks moving in mass formation could be, the history of the campaign of 1940, and thus of whole of the second world war, might have been very different. One of the reasons why the attack through the Ardennes in May 1940 which totally destabilised and defeated the French and British armies worked so well was that the Germans never had to worry about attacks on their supply lines. They might not have had this assurance if the French had had at their disposal an armed force of the type envisaged by de Gaulle.

This is not to say that the Germans would have been defeated. One of the themes which recurs most frequently in de Gaulle's writings on warfare is the unpredictability of what can happen on the battle field. There was no place, in the kind of force envisaged in *Vers l'armée de métier*, for the use of dive bombers as mobile artillery, or indeed of air power in a tactical role at all. De Gaulle himself was so conscious of this omission that in 1944, in an edition of *Vers l'armée de métier* published in Algiers, he altered the original text to make up for it; only to decide to go back in the 1971 edition to what he had first written.[6]

De Gaulle did well in the battle of France. On May 28, with only 140 tanks at his disposal, he fought one of the few successful engagements of the war near Abbeville, and took 200 prisoners. He might have done even better if the rest of the French tank force, which in numbers was almost equal to that of the Germans, had not been under wraps near Toulouse. They were presumably there, if a deliberate act of sabotage is excluded, waiting to be brought into action when the German attack had been held, as it had been in 1914, and they could be used to support infantry in the way the official doctrine commanded.

1940–58

When de Gaulle went to England on June 16, his official position was that of sous-secrétaire d'État à la guerre et à la défense nationale, the equivalent of a junior minister in a British government. He had been appointed to it on June 5 by Paul Reynaud (1878–1966), who had become Président du Conseil on March 19, and under whom he would have been happy to serve if Reynaud had been able to continue in office and been willing to continue the war. But Reynaud had been seriously injured in a car accident, and there seemed to be nobody else available.

On June 17, 1940, the day before his famous broadcast, de Gaulle sent a telegram to General Coulson, minister for war in Pétain's cabinet, asking him for orders, and on June 20 sent another telegram to Bordeaux, where the French government had sought refuge from the Germans, indicating his willingness to serve under General Weygand or 'any other French figure prepared to resist'. He may, initially, have been a man who felt that greatness had been thrust upon him because there was nobody else to play the role which he felt compelled to assume. But it did not take him long to become the historic personage who, like Julius Caesar, spoke and wrote of himself in the third person.

Few great leaders have started off with a lower power base than de Gaulle. He had virtually no money, and was totally reliant on Churchill. Since the French ambassador to Great Britain had resigned and gone to live in Brazil, he could not even use the French Embassy. Initially, 300 or so French servicemen came to join him, including the whole male population of the Île de Sein, just off the coast of Brittany, presumably leaving the women and children to cope as best they could until the end of the war. By the end of 1940, he still had fewer than 3,000 men under his command, and except for Maurice Schumann, not a single politician, trade union leader, churchman or senior military figure had come to join him.

The Vichy régime had been recognised as the legitimate government of France by the United States of America, who saw it as merely one more in the series of administrations to have taken power in France under the Third Republic. The Soviet Union, who had merely had a chargé d'affaires in Paris before May, 1940, upgraded its representation to that of a full ambassador. This was mainly because the Soviet Union had signed a non-aggression pact with Nazi Germany on August 23, 1940. Both the German occupying authorities and the Vichy régime were allowing the French Communist Party newspaper *L'Humanité* to reappear. But the Soviet Union's decision also reflected the standard diplomatic practice of recognising the government which is in effective control of the country. Even the British government never formally declared war on what had officially become L'État français. It recognised the Vichy government, and kept a diplomatic representative there.

The two major turning points for the history of the second world war were the German invasion of Russia on June 21, 1941, and the Japanese attack on Pearl Harbor on December 7 of the same year. It was the former event which was initially more important for de Gaulle. In September 1941, the USSR established contact with him, and the French Communist Party began to support the resistance movement. The United States was much slower to offer support to de Gaulle, partly because Roosevelt saw him as a military adventurer. It was not until July 13, 1944 that Le Conseil National de la Résistance, which had officially declared itself the Gouvernement Provisoire de la République Française on June 3, was finally recognised by the United States as qualified to administer France. De Gaulle was not informed in advance either when D-Day was, or where the allied forces were to land on June 6, 1944.

De Gaulle himself did not land in France until June 14. He then made a rapid visit to the United States and Canada, and returned in August to go directly to Paris. His first action was to go, not as tradition and some of his more enthusiastic left-wing supporters suggested, directly to the Hôtel de Ville in order to stand on the balcony and proclaim the existence of the Republic, as Gambetta had done on September 4, 1870. It was to go to the war office in the rue Saint Dominique. In his view, the Republic had never ceased to exist so there was no point in proclaiming it. Vichy had never been anything but a totally illegal interlude. In the ministry, as he described in a memorable page of the third volume of his war memoirs, *Le Salut*, he found the offices exactly as he had left them in June 1940. Not a paper was out of place, not a chair had been moved. It was a physical illustration of what Article 5 of the 1958 Constitution of the Fifth Republic was to call 'la continuité de l'État', and which it is the responsibility of the president to ensure and protect.

Fourteen years were nevertheless to elapse before de Gaulle could establish the Fifth Republic. After the euphoria of the Liberation, the unanimous election of de Gaulle on November 13, 1945 as head of the provisional government of the Republic and the declaration that he had 'bien mérité de la patrie', they were years in which his disappointment and frustration were even greater than they had been in the 1930s. He had, especially from 1943 onwards, tasted power and been confirmed in his suspicion that he liked it. His provisional government had carried out a programme of nationalisation comparable to the one shortly to be undertaken by the Labour Party under Clement Attlee in

Great Britain, and established the social security system which was to be the basis for the welfare state in France. But the constitution which emerged from a series of elections and referenda in 1945 and 1946 was to all intents and purposes the same as that of the Third Republic which had collapsed in the summer of 1940.

It, too, was a *régime d'assemblée* in which the president of the Republic was once again a figurehead without real power and governments were at the mercy of the political parties. Much to de Gaulle's annoyance, these swiftly re-emerged, albeit occasionally under different names and with different programmes, but seemed fated not to be able to agree with one another. On January 20, 1946, de Gaulle resigned, leaving power, as he put it, 'comme un homme moralement intact', and visibly available to be called upon to solve the problems which, in his view, would inevitably arise and prevent France from being properly governed.

There were problems, and the régime's failure to solve the most important of them, that of Algeria, was to lead to its collapse. Its insistence, between 1946 and 1954, on fighting a war in order to try to keep Indochina as part of the French empire, absorbed roughly the same amount of money as France received under the Marshall Plan of June 1947. But this was to be ended in August 1954 by a civilian politician, Pierre Mendès France, whose only departure from normal constitutional practice of the time was to refuse to count the votes of the communist députés when forming his majority.

The plan for economic recovery drawn up in 1945 by Jean Monnet, and applied by the ever-efficient French civil service, enabled France to recover from the destruction of the second world war with surprising speed. This recovery was not on the scale of that achieved by the Federal Republic of Germany, and the France of the early 1950s was very different from the country produced by the economic miracle which followed de Gaulle's return to power in 1958. But the Fourth Republic was by no means the inadequate régime presented in the speeches made by de Gaulle after the creation of the Rassemblement du Peuple Français in April 1947.

It was not his denunciation of the Communist Party as 'le parti de l'étranger' which saved the Fourth Republic from being overthrown from within. It was the decision by the socialist minister of the interior, Jules Moch, to purge the special riot police, the Compagnies Républicaines de Sécurité, of the members of the French Communist Party who had initially been in a majority when the CRS were set up in 1944. It was this which enabled the governments of the Fourth Republic to use the CRS so effectively against the street violence organised by le Parti Communiste Français, especially at the time of the *grèves insurrectionelles* (politically motivated strikes aimed at destroying the régime) of November 1947.

Like the Third Republic, the Fourth Republic of 1946–58 did a good job for France. It was, it is true, the subject of a certain amount of mockery. Between 1951 and 1958, the walls of the Paris Métro were decorated with an advertisement for Ripolin paint. It showed three large sandwich men, the first bearing the Roman numeral I, the second the Roman numeral II and the third the Roman numeral III, striding confidently along. Behind them, running, came a fourth, smaller sandwich man, bearing the number IV. The slogan ran 'Les Républiques passent. La peinture Ripolin demeure' (Republics pass. Ripolin paint stays), while out of the mouth of the fourth little man came a balloon carrying the words 'Encore une couche' (another layer). But the French have a proverb to the effect that 'il n'y a que le provisoire qui dure' (only the provisional lasts); and without the Algerian problem, the Fourth Republic might still exist today.

Its failure to solve this problem is in marked contrast to its successes in foreign and European policy. De Gaulle's insistence that France had remained a major power despite the defeat of 1940 meant that she had a permanent seat on the Security Council of the United Nations and a zone to administer in occupied Germany between 1945 and 1951. France was thus in a position to support the American decision to go to the aid of South Korea when it was invaded by heavily armed forces from the communist north on June 25, 1950, and French units, under the flag of the United States, took part in the war which finally held the communist armies to a draw in the fighting which continued until 1953.

Although France had few aircraft at its disposal, it played an honourable part in the first victory of the Western powers in the Cold War, the airlift by which, between June 1948 and May 1949, they defeated the Soviet blockade of Berlin. On April 4, 1949, France was one of the twelve countries which signed the Treaty of Washington establishing the North Atlantic Treaty Organization, a decision opposed not only by the French Communist Party but by a large number of left-wing intellectuals. Indeed, the performance of the governments of the Fourth Republic in foreign policy is all the more praiseworthy when one considers how strong the current of opinion was in favour of a neutralist 'third way' approach to the struggle between the Soviet union and the Western democracies. Even *Le Monde*, whose creation de Gaulle himself had encouraged in 1944, was distinctly luke warm in its attitude towards the policies which finally won the Cold War.

Perhaps the best measure of the success of the Fourth Republic, and of its acceptability to the majority of the population, lay in its ability to resist the two most powerful political formations ranged against it, le Parti Communiste Français and de Gaulle's Rassemblement du Peuple Français. On August 30, 1954, these mutually hostile parties joined to make a major contribution to the defeat of the bill confirming the creation of the European Defence Community. On May 17, 1952, Belgium, France, Italy, the Federal Republic of Germany, Luxembourg and the Netherlands had signed the Treaty of Paris establishing a European Army. But the treaty had to be ratified by the parliaments of the six member states, and was held up for two years by France. It was opposed by the Gaullists, as well as by the right wing generally, because of its ambition to rearm Germany, and by the French Communist Party because this was what the Soviet Union had told it to do.

In the event, the defeat of the bill turned out to be a great service to Europe. It ensured that the Americans, who alone had the power to counter-balance that of the Soviet Union, remained in Europe to defend it. And it led, by way of compensation for the supporters of European unification, to the signing on March 25, 1957 of the Treaty of Rome establishing the European Economic Community. France had already, on April 18, 1951, signed the Treaty of Paris establishing the European Coal and Steel Community, the starting point for all future European integration, and these first steps towards a united Europe are yet another indication that the Fourth Republic was a far more stable and efficient régime than de Gaulle would ever officially allow.

His decision, on May 6, 1953, to dissolve the RPF was an implicit recognition of this. The Rassemblement du Peuple Français had, initially, been very successful, and won 40 per cent of the votes cast in the local government elections of October 1947. But in the legislative elections of June 17, 1947, it had won only 121 seats out of a total membership of 610 in the Chambre des Députés, and a number of senior members were preparing to disobey de Gaulle and take office in one of the governments of the Fourth Republic.

There was never any question of Charles de Gaulle trying to seize power by taking to the streets, and he was not, with his solid background in the bourgeoisie of northern France, a military adventurer and womaniser like the two Napoleons. He was equally unlike his first mentor, Philippe Pétain, a notorious philanderer who is said to have enjoyed his last act of physical love at the age of 84, nor did he indulge in the extra-marital relationships which have bestowed their strange immortality on Félix Faure or Georges Boulanger. On April 6, 1921 at the age of 31, de Gaulle had married Yvonne Vendroux, the daughter of a biscuit manufacturer from Calais, who was just ten years his junior. They had three children. Philippe, born December 21, 1921, who entered the navy and became an admiral. Elizabeth, born on May 15, 1924, who married Alain de Boissieu, who had a distinguished military career and became Grand Chancelier de la Légion d'Honneur. And Anne, born on January 1, 1928, who suffered severely from Down's Syndrome.

This was, understandably, the great tragedy of de Gaulle's private life. He was one of the few people who could make contact with her, and she was particularly fond of sitting on his knee and playing with his army *képi*. She died on February 6, 1948, and was buried in the churchyard at Colombey-les-deux-Églises, where de Gaulle had restored the country house of La Boisserie and made it his family home in the 1930s. After the ceremony, when Yvonne de Gaulle was unable to drag herself away from the graveside, her husband took her gently by the arm with the words: 'Come along. She is like everyone else now'. Her death was followed by the establishment of the Fondation Anne de Gaulle, for handicapped children, and all the royalties from de Gaulle's books were given to it. This had the effect, after de Gaulle's death, of leaving Yvonne de Gaulle so short of money that a special fund had to be opened to enable her to spend the rest of her life in dignity.

Without the drama of the Algerian war, de Gaulle would in all probability have slipped into a rather disappointed old age. This would have delighted Yvonne de Gaulle, who is reported to have said 'Nous aurions été si heureux si Charles n'avait pas eu toutes ces idées' (We should have been so happy if Charles had not had all these ideas),[7] and liked nothing better than a little quiet gardening at La Boisserie. The absence of the Algerian problem would also, in all probability, have allowed the Fourth Republic to survive as long as the Third had done before it (1870–1940). The amiable, modest, moderately left-wing politician Vincent Auriol had been elected to the Presidency on January 16, 1947. He rolled his 'r's in a manner typical of the South of France, was described by a former minister of the Third Republic, Anatole de Monzie, as 'un fanatique de la tolérance', behaved with impeccable dignity in public, and led a quiet, bourgeois life at the Élysée palace, where he was known to teach Latin to his grand-children.

The presidential election of December 1953, did not, it is true, show the Fourth Republic in its best light. As in the case of the Third Republic, the president was elected by the body officially known as Le Parlement, and constituted by the Assemblée Nationale, which in the Third Republic was known as the Chambre des Députés, and the Conseil de la République, the name given in the Constitution of 1946 to what in the Third Republic had been called Le Sénat. The successful candidate had to have obtained over 50 per cent of the votes cast by all the députés and members of the Conseil de la République, who together formed what for that occasion was also referred to as Le Congrès.

It took thirteen votes before René Coty (1882–1962) was finally elected, and the dignity of the office was not enhanced by the fact that sweepstakes on the result were being conducted in most of the cafés in France. In the event, the election of Coty brought to the Élysée a man of irreproachable morality, a businessman and maritime lawyer from Normandy, who had had a long career in politics and was conscious of the need to reform a system which was about to be faced with one of the most serious crises ever to confront a democratic régime in France. His conviction that only one person was able to solve this crisis helped to bring Charles de Gaulle back to power, and gave the events of 1958 a greater legality than they actually had.

1958–62

The problem of Algeria began to dominate French politics from the moment when, on the night of October 31, 1954, the Front de Libération Nationale began its armed rebellion. Initially, the FLN probably represented between 1 and 2 per cent of the Arab-speaking population, and its first victim was a 23-year-old French school teacher, Guy Monnerot. The French conquest of Algeria dated from 1830, and in 1848 the Second Republic officially declared it to be part of France and divided it into the three Départements of Algiers, Oran and Constantine. On October 24, 1870, its Jewish inhabitants were offered French citizenship, but this was not extended to the Arab-speaking, Muslim population.

It was the decision to make Algeria *une colonie de peuplement* which made it so hard for the French to decolonise in the way the British had in India or Malaysia, or were to do in most parts of Africa. By 1954, there were over a million permanent French-speaking inhabitants, as against some 9 million Muslims who had almost all remained native speakers of Arabic. The European population, many of whose families had originally come from Italy, Spain or Malta, had roughly the same standard of living as in the poorer parts of southern France or the south of Spain. The Arab-speakers were just above the level of the population of Egypt or the richer parts of India. The nickname for the French settlers was *les pieds noirs*. They could afford boots or shoes. The Arab-speakers went barefoot; or, if they were rich enough, wore sandals.

Both before and after the beginning of the rebellion on November 1, 1954, the *pieds noirs* saw it as the duty of the French state to protect them. Many had served in the French army, and none of them had any intention of allowing themselves to be driven out of their country by the terrorist tactics used by the FLN. By 1956, these tactics had proved so successful than France had been forced to move about half a million soldiers into Algeria to try to protect the civilian population. Most of them were conscripts, whose main ambition, like that of conscripts everywhere, was to become undamaged ex-servicemen as soon as possible. But many of their officers, as well as the members of the crack parachute regiments, had a different ambition. They wanted to win a war, something which the French army had not done by itself since the victories of the first Napoleon in the early years of the nineteenth century.

On May 13, afraid of being abandoned by Paris, and rightly suspecting that the mass of the French population would not be too unhappy to see this happen, a group of French *colons* (settlers), headed by two army officers, General Massu and General Salan, seized the government buildings in Algiers and proclaimed the existence of a comité de salut public. De Gaulle probably knew what was going on, but was not personally involved. On May 6, 1953, he had dissolved the RPF, and seemed resigned to ending his days quietly at Colombey-les-deux-Églises.

Without the events of May 13 he would probably have done so, and must have been delighted to hear that at a subsequent rally in Algiers, on May 15, a civilian activist called Léon Delbecque had cried 'Vive de Gaulle', and that his cry had been taken up by General Salan as well as by the crowd. On May 19, de Gaulle held a press conference at which he declared that he was 'ready to assume the powers of the Republic', a form of words indicating that he was not going to behave as Philippe Pétain had done in July 1940 and create a new, authoritarian régime.

On June 1, 1958, at the urgent request of René Coty, who feared a military putsch in France followed by civil war, de Gaulle agreed to form a government. He appeared before the Assemblée Nationale, a 67-year-old man sitting quite alone in civilian clothes on one of the front benches, and became Président du Conseil des Ministres with 329 votes in his favour and 224 against. His main concern was not Algeria, and his habit of telling whoever came to see him whatever he thought that person wanted to hear, suggests that he had no fixed ideas on the subject. What interested him was the drafting of a new constitution, and he had made his views clear as early as June 16, 1946, in a speech given at Bayeux, the first French town to be liberated in 1944.

These were given definitive form in the Constitution of the Fifth Republic, presented to the French people on September 4, 1958, a date which may have been chosen because it was the eighty-eighth anniversary of the declaration of the Third Republic in 1870. In the referendum of September 28, 1958 there were 17,668,790 votes for the new constitution, 4,624,511 against, and 4,006,614 abstentions, a majority of 80 per cent of those voting, but only 62 per cent of the total electorate. The essential feature of the new constitution was the strengthening of the government in its relationship with parliament and the limiting of the latter's powers. The president was no longer to be elected solely by parliament, as he had been under the Third and Fourth Republics, but by an electoral college of some 80,000 *notables*. These were to include, in addition to members of what now became known as the Assemblée Nationale and the Sénat, a majority of locally elected officials such as mayors and local councillors (conseillers municipaux).

Under the Fifth Republic, the president is thus no longer an emanation of parliament. He has the moral authority stemming from being elected quite separately, and in October 1962 a 'yes' vote at another referendum strengthened this aspect of his position even more. Since then, the president has been elected by universal suffrage. He holds office for seven years, and is eligible for re-election. Like the president of the United States, he is not politically responsible to the legislative body. He can be removed only on conviction of the charge of high treason. Among his duties he appoints the prime minister, can dissolve the Assemblée Nationale, and at moments of national emergency can invoke Article 16 to assume special powers. In accordance with the principle of the separation of powers, députés becoming ministers have to give up their seat, and hand it over to the person known as their *suppléant*. Their loyalty, at least in theory, is to the government of which they are members, not to the party they represent in parliament.

This new constitution did not mean that France ceased to be a parliamentary democracy. The president has no power to make laws. This remains with parliament. Only parliament has the right to raise taxes. The judiciary, as in the United States, is independent both of the executive and the legislative branches of government. The accusations formulated against the Constitution of the Fifth Republic by left-wing and liberal thinkers in 1958 have proved wrong. It has not produced a dictatorship. It was nevertheless clearly made for de Gaulle, who was elected by a comfortable majority by the Collège des Notables as its first president on December 21, 1958.

On January 8, 1959, de Gaulle took over from René Coty, who had saluted his election with the remark 'le premier des Français est maintenant le premier en France'. The main problem which the new president had to tackle was obviously that of Algeria, where de Gaulle proceeded to do exactly the opposite of what everybody expected. For the army and the European settlers in Algeria, de Gaulle was the man to keep Algeria French. He was, after all, a soldier, a nationalist, a Catholic, the man who had kept French honour alive between 1940 and 1944. He had also included in Article 2 of the Constitution of 1958 the traditional insistence on a Republic which was 'indivisible'. No part, at least in theory, could be separated from the others and given away. The left, and the intellectual establishment generally, made the same predictions as the army and settlers as to how he would behave. De Gaulle, it was argued, would be inevitably led to install a more authoritarian, semi-dictatorial régime in France, since there was no other way of putting the policy of L'Algérie Française, which they were certain he would pursue, into action.

Initially, it looked as though de Gaulle would fulfil the expectations of both his critics and his admirers. On June 4, 1958, he visited Algeria, and addressed the crowd in the forum in Algiers. As he raised his arms in the characteristic gesture which transformed his whole body into a vast V for Victory sign, and proclaimed 'Algériens, je vous ai compris', everyone went delirious with excitement. It was only gradually that the true meaning of his words became apparent. It was not 'I have understood you, and will do everything to ensure that Algeria remains French'. It was 'I understand your desire to keep Algeria French. But, sorry lads, it's not on'.

After giving priority to the re-establishment of order in Algeria, where the number of terrorist attacks fell dramatically, and the need for the French army to torture suspects declined accordingly, de Gaulle went on television on September 16, 1959, to offer three solutions to the Algerian problem. These were secession; total integration with France; and what was clearly his own preference, *l'association*. Three months later, when the full implication of these proposals had sunk in, they led to the first test of Gaulle's authority when General Massu gave an interview on January 18, 1959 to the mass circulation German newspaper *Süddeutsche Zeitung* in which he said that the army had perhaps made a mistake in supporting de Gaulle, and might have to think again.

Massu was immediately dismissed from his post, and summoned to Paris, where he had a furious argument with de Gaulle. On January 24, the European activists in Algeria ordered a general strike, and a group of them occupied the university buildings. When the regular police and the gendarmes mobiles moved against them, shots were fired, fourteen policemen and eight demonstrators were killed, and some 200 people wounded. De Gaulle, suspecting that the European rebels were not powerful enough to take over the whole city, and knowing that there was no second de Gaulle waiting in the wings, bided his time.

On January 29, 1959, in full military uniform, he appeared on television. Speaking, as he said, 'en vertu du mandat que le peuple m'a confié et de la légitimité nationale que j'incarne depuis vingt ans' (by virtue of the mandate entrusted to me by the people and of the national legitimacy which I have incarnated for twenty years), he appealed to the nation to support him, and ordered the rebels to surrender. On February 1, they did so, and de Gaulle had won the first round. As in the second world war, when the microphone had been the only weapon with which he could reply to the German tanks, his victory in January 1960 appeared at first sight to be first and foremost a demonstration of the efficacy of the mass media and a triumph of public relations.

There were, however, other factors, including de Gaulle's strength of will, his charisma as a military leader, and the fact that by 1959, the climate of opinion had visibly begun to change in France. Few people in metropolitan France had ever really cared very much about Algeria, and the main concern of most families now was to see their sons come home from service there as soon as possible. But before the return to power of de Gaulle in the summer of 1958, few French politicians had had the courage or perhaps even the inclination to say that French Algeria was a lost cause. The campaign against L'Algérie Française had been led essentially by writers and intellectuals, by men of such different political persuasion as Raymond Aron and Jean-Paul Sartre, in journals such as *Témoignage chrétien*, *Le Monde*, and the left-wing *France Observateur*. Now it was being led, implicitly if not yet with complete openness, by the hero of the second world war.

One of the major criticisms of the referendum of September 28, 1958, by which the Constitution of the Fifth Republic was given legal status, was that it was really a plebiscite in favour of de Gaulle, held in the shadow of the threat of a military *coup d'état* which had already taken place and might be repeated if the electorate gave the wrong answer. Similar criticisms were voiced of the referenda of January 8, 1961 and April 8, 1962, whereby de Gaulle obtained and retained public support for his policy on Algeria.

The referendum of January 8, 1961 was also criticised for the form in which the question was put. To ask the French people if it 'approved the Bill submitted by the President of the Republic concerning the self-determination of the Algerian populations and the organisation of the public powers in Algeria before self-determination' was, it was argued, to confuse two separate issues. You could not say that you wanted Algerian independence, and thus an end to the war, without confirming de Gaulle in the possession of constitutional powers which you might well regard as excessive and undemocratic.

The referendum of April 8, 1962 confirming the Evian agreements negotiated in the summer of the previous year, and by which Algeria was to become independent, was not open to the same criticism, and 90 per cent of those voting said 'yes' as opposed to 75 per cent in January 1961. While this may have been because the question was not so ambiguous, a more likely explanation is that the attempt at a further *coup d'état* in Algeria, which had taken place a year earlier, in April 1961, had reminded the French people of how great the risk of civil war still was, and of how totally they relied on de Gaulle to prevent it from breaking out.

On April 21, 1961, Generals Challe, Zeller, Jouhaud and Salan seized power in Algeria. Marshal Juin, who had been born in Algeria and who had, in January 1960, gone to see de Gaulle in order to plead the cause of the European settlers, remained discreetly in the background. General Olié, Chief of the French General Staff in Algeria, left Paris in the company of Louis Joxe, the minister for Algerian affairs, to rally support for the government. While the parachute regiments tended to support what de Gaulle called 'un quarteron de généraux en retraite' (a gang of four retired generals), the mass of the army offered no support for the attempted take-over.

This may have been because they were put off by the Cold War rhetoric used by the four rebellious generals, who asked whether France really wanted Mers-el-Kébir and Algiers to be 'tomorrow's bases for the Soviet Union'. It was more probably because they wanted to go home, and could use their newly invented transistor radios to listen to what de Gaulle said and to follow what was happening in France itself. As in January 1960, de Gaulle had put on his uniform and appeared on television. His speech of Sunday April 23 calling upon the rebels to surrender was one of his great performances, and effectively settled the issue as far as public opinion in France was concerned.

Neither in parliament, nor in the trade union movement, nor in educational circles, was there any support for whatever Challe, Jouhaud, Zeller and Salan were trying to do, and even they seemed uncertain as to what their final objectives were. De Gaulle's first prime minister, Michel Debré, had been known before 1958 as one of the most eloquent defenders of L'Algérie Française. By appointing him as head of a government whose long-term objective was to give Algeria its independence, de Gaulle ensured that the policy of L'Algérie Française was publicly rejected in the person of one of its leading proponents. Debré had always been a devoted Gaullist, and could not refuse to do what his hero asked him to do.

It was a master stroke of the Machiavellian style leadership which de Gaulle had openly admired in 1927, and which reached its culmination on the night of April 22, 1961. For then it was Michel Debré who had to go on the radio to urge the inhabitants of Paris to climb into their cars and drive to the airports where the paratroops from Algeria were expected to land, and, as he put it, 'convince these misguided soldiers how great their error was'. Debré looked even more of a fool when it transpired that de Gaulle's broadcast of April 21 had already begun to defuse the situation. By April 25, the generals' rebellion had collapsed, their ultimate humiliation taking place when they tried to harangue the crowd in the forum in Algiers, only to discover that somebody had turned off the electricity, without which the loud-speakers would not work.

The danger of civil war had nevertheless been very real. The conscripts may have listened on their transistors, and realised that their senior officers had no support in metropolitan France. But only de Gaulle had the charisma and moral authority which ensured that he would be obeyed by the paratroopers and the middle-ranking, career officers who had to accept the orders of a head of state who had himself been a soldier, who was in uniform, and who had saved the honour of France in 1940. The supporters of L'Algérie Française were certainly in a minority, but one which could still do immense harm. Both before and after the referendum of April 8, 1962 and the official proclamation of Algerian independence, a European-based terrorist group known as L'Organisation de l'Armée Secrète, exercised a reign of terror in France itself as well as in Algeria, and did more damage than the FLN had done during the seven and a half years of warfare.

De Gaulle was lucky. The proclamation of Algerian independence on July 1, 1962 came in the middle of one of the great periods of growth for the French economy. Much emphasis had been placed on the fate of the million or so European settlers, most of whom had known no other home but Algeria, and for whom there was no place in a country dominated by their enemies. They clearly did not believe the articles in the Evian agreements putting an end to the war, and which guaranteed them a place in the newly-independent Algeria. They believed their own politicians, who had told them during the whole of the war that a victory for the FLN meant that they had only one choice: either the coffin or the suitcase.

To the apparent surprise of the French government, which seems to have had a greater belief than the *pieds noirs* in the promises of the FLN, over 800,000 of them decided to come to France. Initially, not more than 100,000 had been expected, and there was some doubt as to what term should be used to describe them. Georges Pompidou, who had taken over as prime minister on April 14, 1962, is said to have called them 'des déportés'. It was a term with too many associations with what the Germans had done to the Jews in France between 1940 and 1944 to be officially adopted. It nevertheless reflected the attitude of most of the *pieds noirs* to what was happening to them more accurately than the expression finally adopted of 'des rapatriés'. Few of them had even been to France, let alone lived there as in their own country.

Another past participle, 'des repliés', would have been equally accurate. The verb 'se replier' is used when an army decides to 'withdraw to previously prepared positions'. Although the French army had won the Algerian war on the ground, in the sense that by the end of 1961 most of the country was effectively under its control, and not under that of the FLN, the *pieds noirs* were victims of a political defeat, and the linguistically odd expression of 'des repliés' was quite accurate. Fortunately there were on July 7, 1962 only 21,000 jobless in France, a fact which made the end of the Algerian war far more of a tragedy for Algeria than for the now exiled *pieds noirs*.

Alain Peyrefitte, de Gaulle's minister of information from 1962 to 1966, quotes de Gaulle as summarising the main reason for France leaving Algeria in the phrase 'Bye, bye, vous nous coûtez trop cher' (Bye, bye, you are too expensive). He also, however, attributes him with a more ambitious motive when he quotes him as saying that Europe, presumably in the sense of the European Economic Community, offered France 'le moyen devenir ce qu'elle a cessé d'être depuis Waterloo, la première au monde' (The opportunity of becoming what she had ceased to be at Waterloo, the first nation in the world).[8]

If one neglects the hyperbole, it is possible to see what de Gaulle meant, and to recognise him as seeing where France's true interests lay. The French had never been as interested as the British in building an overseas empire. They had had no Kipling, and in 1759 one of their greatest writers, Voltaire, had dismissed the Seven Years War of 1756–63 as a quarrel over 'quelques arpents de neige vers le Canada' (a few acres of snow over towards Canada).[9] On April 30, 1803, under the Louisiana purchase, Napoleon I had sold what is now Arkansas, the Dakotas, Iowa, Kansas, Missouri, Montana, Nebraska and Oklahoma to the United States for 15 million dollars, roughly 4 cents an acre.

Since Napoleon then proceeded to waste several times that sum, to say nothing of the lives of half a million men, in his 1812 invasion of Russia, it was not a very sensible move. It nevertheless underlined how France's historical destiny had already become a European one, and it was a choice which de Gaulle confirmed by agreeing to give up Algeria. It was, in a broader historical context as well as in the immediate circumstances of 1962, as great a service to his country as his decision to fly to London and continue the war in June 1940, if not a greater one. In 1940, he had shown the quality of his historical and political vision by recognising that the war which had begun in 1939 was indeed a world war, and not merely a third episode in the essentially European conflict between France and Germany. He was now showing comparable wisdom in recognising that France's destiny lay in Europe, not in her overseas empire.

The prosperity of the 1960s enabled the *pieds noirs* to be absorbed relatively painlessly into France. Until the increase in unemployment in the 1970s and 1980s led to the rise of Jean-Marie Le Pen's Front National, there was little by way of an irredentist party to threaten the security of the republic. At the same time, an apparently irresistible demographic explosion, bringing the population to 18 million by 1980 and to an apparently inevitable 28 million by the end of the century, made economic growth impossible in Algeria. In France, the continuation of unparalleled economic growth was accompanied by monetary and political stability. For the first time in its history, it had lost a war but won the peace.

1962–70

The Algeria problem solved, de Gaulle turned once again to the question of the Constitution. The 1947 Discours de Bayeux, the starting point for the Constitution of the Fifth Republic, had given no details as to how the president was to be elected. It merely said that the head of state was 'placé au-dessus de partis', and de Gaulle's criticism of political parties was not limited to the way they had governed France under the Third and Fourth republics. In the 1960s, the Federal Republic of Germany was far and away the most prosperous country in Europe. This did not prevent de Gaulle from saying that it had a bad constitution, in the sense of one which had been invented and imposed on the country by the English and the Americans, which gave all power to the political parties, and which forbade the use of the referendum.[10]

On October 28, 1962, de Gaulle organised what turned out to be his last successful attempt to have a proposal endorsed by the French people in a referendum. His aim was to change the mode of election of the president of the Republic, and 12,809,607 voters said 'yes' to the proposal that this should be by universal suffrage and no longer by an electoral college, while 7,032,695 said 'no'. But there were 6,280, 297 abstentions, and it was his least successful use of the referendum so far, foreshadowing the defeat in the referendum of April 27, 1969 which led to his resignation.

In 1962 de Gaulle also had in mind the fact the next presidential election was due to take place in 1965, and that there was no certainty that the 80,000 *notables* would chose him over one of his potential rivals, the provincial businessman and conservative politician Antoine Pinay (1891–1994). He was almost exactly de Gaulle's age, and there were other factors which suggested that the 80,000 *illustres inconnus* might prefer one of their own.

De Gaulle had done what he had basically been called back to power to do – solved the Algerian problem. The introduction of le nouveau franc in January 1, 1959, and the consequent conversion of the francs of the Fourth Republic into centimes, had been accompanied by a policy of sound money which had kept inflation down and the working class more or less in order. This was what Pinay had already done under the Fourth Republic during the nine months in which he had been Président du Conseil, from March 6 to December 23, 1952, as well as in the longer period in which he had continued in office as minister of finance. He was, moreover, clearly a believer in party politics as traditionally practised in France. So were the 80,000 *notables*. De Gaulle, equally obviously, was not.

The immediate explanation which de Gaulle gave for the referendum of October 28, 1962 was that he had almost fallen victim to the assassination attempt of August 22, 1962 carried out by members of the Organisation de l'Armée Secrète. In his view, this was a reminder of the need to put the final touch on the Constitution of the Fifth Republic by having the president elected by universal suffrage, though it is hard to follow his logic here. There was no accompanying proposal to see the introduction of a vice-president on the American model, and thus have someone immediately on hand to take over as Lyndon B. Johnson took over when John Kennedy was assassinated on November 22, 1963. For most journalists and politicians, the basic reason lay partly in de Gaulle's obvious desire to be re-elected in 1965, but also in what looked at times like an almost neurotic need to be told by the French people that they still loved him.

There was a great deal of opposition to the proposal. On October 4, 280 out of the 465 members of the Assemblée Nationale had expressed it by voting a motion of no confidence in the government of Georges Pompidou. Instead of doing what would be considered normal in a parliamentary democracy, and asking the government to resign, de Gaulle kept Pompidou's government in office and used the right given to him under Article 12 of the Constitution to dissolve the Assembly. This increased the hostility to the referendum already being expressed by virtually every political party except the Gaullists, and by the majority of newspapers and political commentators.

The president of the Senate, Gaston Monnerville, said that election by universal suffrage would produce 'not the Republic but a kind of enlightened Bonapartism', and described the way the referendum had been proposed as 'une forfaiture', an 'abuse of authority'. The Conseil d'État, the supreme court for administrative law, also criticised the proposal on a number of grounds, but the average voter clearly regarded these objections as mere technicalities. After de Gaulle had won the referendum, he openly supported Pompidou's Union pour la Nouvelle République, which won an overall majority of 229 seats out of 465 in the legislative elections of November 7 and 18, 1962.

Part of de Gaulle's success in the referendum may be due to the fact that it took place on the day that Krushchev ended the most serious crisis of the Cold War by announcing that the Soviet Union would withdraw the missiles which it had secretly installed in Cuba. The sudden increase of the danger of a nuclear war made the French realise how important it was to have a leader with undisputable authority as head of state, and de Gaulle had taken an impeccably hard line. When President Kennedy's special envoy, Dean Acheson, had come to show him the photographs which proved that the Soviet Union had broken its promise not to put nuclear missiles in Cuba, de Gaulle waved them away. The president's word, he assured Acheson, was enough for him. When the Soviet ambassador had warned him of the dangers of nuclear warfare which he claimed had been created by the United States blockade of Cuba, de Gaulle had calmly replied that in that case, they would die together.

According to Alain Peyrefitte, it was de Gaulle's firmness which had been instrumental in dissuading President Eisenhower from yielding in May 1960 to Krushchev's insistence that he apologise for the flight of the U2 reconnaissance planes over the Soviet Union.[11] De Gaulle certainly took a stronger line than Harold Macmillan in the long crisis sparked off by the Soviet Union's threat, on November 28, 1958, to sign a separate peace treaty with East Germany. According to the Soviet Union, the effect of such a treaty would be to put an end to the right of the Western powers to keep their garrisons in West Berlin, a step which would lead to the 2.5 million inhabitants of that city being rapidly absorbed into the communist state set up in the Soviet-occupied zone after 1945.

While Macmillan looked as though he was prepared to compromise, de Gaulle followed the same policy as the one adopted by the Fourth Republic at the time of the Berlin blockade of 1948. There was, in his view, no case for any kind of change, and there is an instructive contrast between his readiness to support the United States on this issue and the hostility which he showed in the 1960s to both Great Britain and the United States in other contexts. It may well be that de Gaulle was right, and while American policy towards the Soviet Union was correct in Europe, it was out of place in Vietnam and elsewhere. Another explanation may lie in the fact that support for the people of West Berlin was essential to what was becoming the main plank in French foreign policy, the development of increasingly good relations with the Federal Republic of Germany.

In July 1962, Konrad Adenauer had made a state visit to France, and had stood side by side with de Gaulle to watch French and German soldiers marching and manoeuvring together. At Rheims cathedral, on July 8, de Gaulle gave a moving speech announcing the end of the long hostility which had caused three wars between the two countries in under 100 years. On January 22, 1963, a week after de Gaulle's announcement at a press conference that France was vetoing Great Britain's application to join the European Economic Community, the formal signature of a treaty of co-operation between France and the Federal Republic of Germany officially inaugurated a policy which has remained constant to the present day. The *franc fort* policy adopted by François Mitterrand in March 1983, and the subsequent linking of the franc to the German mark, is the translation into monetary and economic terms of one of the major political choices made by de Gaulle.

If it had survived the Algerian crisis, it is a choice that might have been made, in less dramatic terms and in a manner which showed less hostility to France's other allies, by one of the governments of the Fourth Republic. The signature on April 18, 1951 of the Treaty of Paris establishing the European Coal and Steel Community, followed on March 25, 1957 by the signature of the Treaty of Rome, had already been decisive steps on the way to a permanent reconciliation between France and Germany. It is, on the other hand, unlikely that any French politician other than de Gaulle would have vetoed Great Britain's application to join the European Economic Community.

It is also hard for anyone except a determined British opponent of the United Kingdom's membership of the EEC to see what useful purpose was served either by the initial veto of January 14, 1963 or by de Gaulle's repetition of it on November 27, 1967. It set France against the other five members, and confirmed the impression that de Gaulle's principal aim was the political one of excluding a power whose political influence could compete with that of France. In spite of the economic recovery which had enabled the Federal Republic of Germany to become the paymaster of the EEC, the Germans had still not quite succeeded in working their way back from Auschwitz and Belsen to the point where they were seen as entitled to play a major political role in Europe, or indeed anywhere else.

On May 15, 1962, de Gaulle had already shown what kind of united Europe he was prepared to accept and what he was not. In one of the press conferences which he was in the habit of using to announce his views, he stated that there was no future for any kind of Europe other than one of sovereign national states, 'l'Europe des Patries'. The terms in which he dismissed the notion of an integrated Europe, saying that neither Dante nor Chateaubriand would have been able to serve European culture if they had written in 'some kind of integrated Esperanto or Volapük', so offended the ministers from the Christian Democrat Mouvement Républicain Populaire whom Pompidou had integrated in an attempt to widen his government, that they immediately resigned. It was an understandable reaction on their part, but a reminder of the fact that in excluding the United Kingdom from the EEC, de Gaulle was depriving himself of a valuable potential ally. The British, after all, were equally opposed to any kind of Europe other than that based on the nation state.

De Gaulle may have been right to base his veto on the idea that the British were anxious to transform the EEC into what he called 'une vaste zone de libre échange', and reducing the influence of the institutions which made it into a customs union.[12] But his attitude in the second crisis in which he set France against the other members of the European Economic Community was not exactly calculated to make it much more than a free trade area. On June 30, 1965, France rejected the Hallstein plan intended to enable the Community to have an autonomous budget. When the other members refused to endorse French objections, which were also aimed against the introduction of a degree of majority voting in the EEC, France implemented the 'empty chair policy'. This involved its representatives staying away from all EEC meetings, and thus making progress on any matter completely impossible. It was only on January 1, 1966, when the 'Luxembourg principle' gave each member state the right to veto any proposal which it judged a threat to its 'vital interests', that France agreed to come back to the table.

It was de Gaulle's description of the United Kingdom as a 'Trojan horse' which made it clear that his main target in the 1963 veto was the United States. Ever since his disagreements with Roosevelt during the second world war, anti-Americanism had been one of the dominant strands in de Gaulle's thinking, and in this respect it is tempting to quote the remark which Jean-François Revel made about him in his 1965 pamphlet *En France*: 'Le général de Gaulle a parfaitement raison de croire qu'il incarne la France, il a tort de croire que cela soit flatteur pour lui' (General de Gaulle is quite right to see himself as the incarnation of France. Where he is mistaken is to believe that this is flattering for him).

The 1960s saw at least three other manifestations of de Gaulle's anti-Americanism. These were his announcement, on March 7, 1966, that French forces would be withdrawn from the joint military command of the North Atlantic Treaty Organisation, and the implementation of this announcement on April 1, 1967; the speech on September 1, 1966, at Phnom Penh, in Cambodia, in which he criticised American intervention in Vietnam; and his address to the crowd from the balcony of the town hall in Montréal in which he pronounced the words 'Vive le Québec libre!'. It was a deliberate appeal to Quebec to secede, and provoked such strong public reaction from the Canadian government that de Gaulle cut short his visit. Whether he seriously wished to recover 'les quelques arpents de neige vers le Canada' lost in the Treaty of Paris in 1763 is not entirely clear.

What was, in contrast, very clear, was the strong echo of the anti-semitism prevalent in France during de Gaulle's early years in his remark about the Jews in his press conference of November 27, 1967.

Before the six-day war of June 5 to June 10, 1967, in which Israeli forces had prevented yet another attempt to destroy the state of Israel, de Gaulle had already given an indication that French policy was moving in the same direction of open hostility to Israel which the Soviet Union had already adopted. On June 2, he had announced an embargo on the shipment of arms to the Middle East, and since France's main client in the area at the time was Israel, there was little doubt as to where de Gaulle's sympathy lay. In other circumstances, his description in his press conference of November 27, 1967 of the Jews as 'un peuple d'élite, sûr de lui et dominateur' might have seemed a compliment to them for being so like the French. In 1967, it was at one and the same time an indirect attack on the United States through one of their principal allies, as well as a sign to the Palestine Liberation Organisation that it would not find any opposition in France to its desire to destroy Israel.

It was the announcement that France was going to withdraw her forces from the NATO command, while still remaining a political member of the alliance, which prompted Lyndon Johnson's exasperated appeal to Maurice Schumann: 'For God's sake, tell me once and for all what General de Gaulle wants'. It also justifies Raymond Aron's comment that de Gaulle's great mistake in foreign policy was to have led the French to make a mistake as to who their real enemy was. Now that the Soviet Union seemed to have given up its attempt to bully the West into giving up Berlin, de Gaulle moved towards the same position which had led him, in June 1942, to threaten to leave London and establish the headquarters of the Free French in Moscow. Between June 20 and July 1, 1966, he paid a much publicised visit to the Soviet Union, in which he became the first foreign head of state to visit the hitherto secret rocket-launching base at Zezdograd, and received President Kossyguin for a nine-day state visit to France in December of the same year.

De Gaulle's speech at Phnom Penh on September 1, 1966 attacking American policy in Vietnam appears in its most favourable light if seen in the context of the announcement on January 27, 1964 that France was establishing diplomatic relations with the Chinese People's Republic. Great Britain had already done this in 1950, while also continuing to recognise the nationalist government in Taiwan, and the French action could be seen as the implementation of the traditional practice of awarding diplomatic recognition to any régime which is effectively in control of the country where it is situated. It is unlikely to have had much influence on President Nixon's decision to recognise the Chinese People's Republic in December 1972, though France could feel a justifiable pride at the fact that the negotiations which eventually led to the end of the Vietnam war in January 1973 were held in Paris. It was, after all, the French insistence on trying to keep their former empire in Indochina between 1946 and 1954 which had led to the situation where the United States intervened in the late 1960s to defend the south against attacks from the communist north.

However eccentric some of de Gaulle's behaviour on the international scene may have become after he had solved the Algerian problem, France never became the kind of rogue state which she had been during the reign of Louis XIV or of Napoleon I. De Gaulle's insistence on developing an independent nuclear deterrent was the prolongation of a policy already adopted by the Fourth Republic. It reflected a suspicion of the United States rather than any actual hostility, and was justified by de Gaulle when he pointed out that in September 1938 Czechoslovakia had had the firmest possible written guarantees by Great Britain and France, but was still swallowed up without struggle by Nazi Germany. There was always the possibility that the United States might decide not to put the safety of Chicago or New York at risk to defend West Berlin, and the French deterrent might then serve as a useful trip-wire.

It is true that there was something faintly comic about de Gaulle's description of French nuclear weapons, on 27 January 1968, as 'une force de frappe tous azimuts'. The idea of France being able to strike at any part of the globe was both technically incredible and politically ridiculous. There was always the temptation, for the French themselves as well as for foreign observers, to laugh at de Gaulle, as well as to laugh with him. He did not lack a sense of humour, and was especially adept at performing the role of a mythical creature called 'de Gaulle'. Indeed, he is even said to have invented a number of anecdotes about himself, including the reply which he made when Jackie Kennedy said to him, with the obvious desire to impress: 'Vous savez, ma mère appartenait à une vieille famille française'. 'La mienne aussi, madame.'

De Gaulle also had a number of minor peculiarities, including so visible an inability to lose gracefully that he had some difficulty finding people to partner him at bridge.[13] If it is indeed true that Yvonne de Gaulle said that their marriage would have been perfect 'si Charles n'avait pas eu toutes ces idées', it is a pity she did not introduce him to golf. As the Oldest Member comments in the P. G. Wodehouse short story, 'The Magic Plus Fours', the great service which golf teaches human beings is that, whatever triumphs they may have achieved in other walks of life, they are after all merely human. It acts as a corrective against sinful pride. I attribute the insane arrogance of the later Roman emperors almost entirely to the fact that, having never played golf, they never knew that strange chastening humility that comes from a topped chip-shot.

In spite of his excellent upbringing, de Gaulle was not always the perfect host. It was not for the food and drink that invitations to the family home of La Boisserie, at Colombey-les-Deux-Églises were so highly prized. It is said that when de Gaulle commented to one of his ministers 'Il paraît que vos buvez beaucoup', he received the swift reply 'Pas chez vous, mon Général' ('They tell me you drink a lot'. 'Not when one of your guests, mon Général'). From his long years as a professional soldier, de Gaulle had kept the habit of eating very quickly. He drank as much wine as the butler, under the watchful eye of Yvonne de Gaulle, was prepared to serve him, devoured the main course, took two helpings of pudding, and was finished. Since the service was rather slow, and all the plates were removed as soon as the General had finished his meal and stood up, it was not unusual for guests to rise from the table as hungry as when they sat down.

De Gaulle's victory in the presidential election which took place by universal suffrage on December 5 and 19, 1965 was less of a walk-over than he had expected, and Jean Lacouture describes him as seriously considering the possibility of giving up when he failed to be elected on the first ballot.[14] De Gaulle was, by all accounts, subject to violent swings of mood, and it was also under the impact of a sudden access of depression that he performed, on May 29, 1968, in the middle of the student rebellion, the one act in his life of which he said that he was ashamed.

At ten-thirty in the morning, he suddenly disappeared, without telling anyone where he was going. At two-fifty, he arrived at Baden Baden, where he had gone to see General Massu. According to Massu himself, this was less because he wanted to know whether the army would be prepared to intervene in order to restore order, than because he needed the moral boost which a few hours' conversation with a fellow soldier could provide. It was nevertheless an action which suggested that he no longer had the sureness of touch which had enabled him to deal with the army's opposition to his Algerian policy in January 1960 and April 1961. The crisis provoked by the student rebellion of May 1968 was effectively dealt with by Georges

Pompidou, and will be studied in more detail in the chapter devoted to de Gaulle's immediate successor to the presidency.

The role which this crisis played in de Gaulle's departure from power on April 28, 1969 lay partly in the demonstration given by *les événements de mai* that there was someone ready and able to take over from him. The threat which had helped him to win the referenda of September 28, 1958, of January 8, 1961, of April 8, 1962 and October 28, 1962 was no longer relevant. He could not, in April 1969, tell the French that it was a choice between him and chaos. The solid, reliable Monsieur Pompidou was there, as safe a pair of hands as the most timorous bourgeois could wish for, as well as a man who was still only 58. De Gaulle, in contrast, was about to celebrate his 79th birthday on November 22, 1969.

There were other factors which explain why de Gaulle lost the referendum of April 27, 1969 by 11,945,149 votes to 10,512,469, with 5,562,396 abstentions. It was, to begin with, rather surprising that de Gaulle, whose attitude towards the government of France had always been in the Jacobin tradition of a strong, centralised state, should be asking the French to approve a certain degree of decentralisation. He was, it was felt, really asking for something else: a general vote of approval of the kind he had received in September 1958, in April 1961 and in October 1962, the reassurance that the French still loved him, and could not live without him.

Among the more politically conscious, there was also the realisation that the proposal to reform the Senate was an attempt by de Gaulle to get his own back on a body which had never given him the whole-hearted support which he wanted. It was Gaston Monnerville (1897–1991), who had been Président du Conseil de la République under the Fourth Republic, from 1947 to 1958, and had then been elected Président du Sénat when the second chamber changed its name with the advent of the Fifth Republic, who had been one of his fiercest critics at the time of the referendum of October 28, 1962.

Under the Constitution of the Fifth Republic, it is the Président du Sénat who takes over on a temporary basis if the president of the Republic is unable to act, and one of the proposals in the referendum of April 28, 1969 was to take this function from him. The Senate itself was to lose its role as second legislative chamber, and take on a purely consultative role. It would thus no longer have the power to vote on parliamentary bills, and the proposal was obviously aimed at strengthening the power of the prime minister and, through him, that of the president who appointed him.

De Gaulle had not given up his detestation for what he called 'les jeux, les poisons et les délices du système', and still saw the organised political parties as responsible for the disaster of 1940. Neither had he forgiven them for having kept him out of power between 1947 and 1958. But the Senate was not a body in which party politics played a major role. Its members kept their seats for nine years, one third being renewed once every three years. They were elected by *les notables*, and therefore tended to represent the provincial, middle-class France which de Gaulle had always disliked.

It is this which explains one of his comments after receiving the news that he had lost the referendum: that it was the revenge of the France which had supported the Vichy régime. In his view, as in that of his great ideological enemy, Jean-Paul Sartre, the working class had never accepted Vichy. The bourgeoisie, on the other hand, had worshipped le maréchal Pétain, and was taking its final revenge on the man who had defied his authority in 1940. They were also taking an opportunity to punish the man who had deprived them, by the referendum of October 28, 1962 which instigated the election of the president of the Republic by universal suffrage, of their power to elect the head of state.

Considerations of this kind were nevertheless unlikely to have been uppermost in the minds of the people who turned out to vote on April 27, 1969. Under the Fifth Republic, as indeed under the Third and Fourth and even more under the Vichy régime, the French radio was under the firm control of the government. This meant that virtually no criticism of de Gaulle was ever heard on the air, and one of the great surprises of the 1965 presidential election had been the sudden discovery by the French, on seeing opposition candidates such as François Mitterrand and Jean Lecanuet on television, that they did not have pointed ears and a visible tail.

When the news came that 53 per cent of those voting in the referendum of April 27, 1969 had said 'no', de Gaulle's reaction to the confirmation that he had indeed become yesterday's man was immediate. At midnight on the same day, he issue a brief communiqué: 'Je cesse d'exercer les fonctions de Président de la République. Cette décision prend effet à minuit'. The president of the Senate, Alain Poher, took over the duties of president on an interim basis, and stood, unsuccessfully, as a candidate against Georges Pompidou. To the delight of Yvonne de Gaulle, her husband went back to Colombey-les-deux-Églises, and she was able to indulge in her passion for gardening in the knowledge that he was safely in the house, writing his *Mémoires d'espoir*, the account of his achievements since coming back to power in 1958.

During the presidential elections of May–June 1969, in which de Gaulle abstained from making public his support for Georges Pompidou, he accompanied his wife to Ireland, where they were the official guests of President de Valera. On June 13, he delivered a speech in which he declared his support for a united Ireland. However, somebody had turned off the microphone. In June 1970, he and his wife visited Spain. On June 8, to the surprise of many of his admirers, 'l'homme du 18 juin' was received by General Franco, the man whom he had so signally failed to resemble after May 13, 1958, and who still had five years to go as dictator. On November 9, 1970, while playing patience in front of the television, waiting for the eight o'clock news bulletin, de Gaulle suddenly died of a heart attack. He was buried, according to his wishes, in the cemetery of Colombey-les-deux-Églises, beside his daughter Anne.

2 Georges Pompidou

The conscientious uncle

1911–46

On July 10, 1940, 569 of the députés and sénateurs of the Third
Republic voted to give full powers to the 84-year-old Marshal Pétain.
A large photograph of him was then printed and posted up
throughout France, bearing the question 'Êtes-vous plus Français que
lui?'. Had Georges Pompidou, at the time awaiting demobilisation as a
lieutenant with the 141st régiment d'infanterie alpine, been interested
enough in the question, he could easily have said that he was at least as
French as 'le Maréchal'. Both his social origins and his career certainly
gave him the right to do so. Had he been endowed with the gift of
prophecy, he could have added that he was going to give much more
valuable service to his country.

Pompidou, whose regiment had just been awarded the croix de
guerre, a decoration awarded only to those showing courage under fire
in the face of the enemy, came from a background which was as
quintessentially French as Pétain's own. He had also, as Pétain had,
started off as a public servant with no advantages except for his own
intelligence and capacity for hard work. Both men were of provincial
peasant stock. Pétain was a farmer's son from the north of France,
who joined the army in 1876, and was promoted on November 18,
1918 to the rank of *maréchal de France*. Georges Pompidou was the
grandson of a *maître valet* (farm labourer) from Auvergne, Jean
Pompidou, who earned 250 gold francs a year, and married a seam-
stress who brought him a dowry of 1,000 francs. With the 2,000 francs
he had saved, this gave him enough money to buy his own house.

Léon Pompidou, his son, belonged to the first generation to profit
from the laws of 1881 and 1882 making primary education free,
compulsory, universal and secular throughout France. On finishing his
studies, he became an *instituteur*, a primary school teacher. It was the

first step in a pattern of social advancement which was to become as quintessentially French as the path which used to take the Minister's son, in Scotland, from the manse to the university, and then to a glittering career in advocacy, business, scholarship or the civil service.

In France, what the journalist Christine Clerc described as the 'cursus légendaire institutionalisé sous la III République'[1] (legendary pattern institutionalised under the Third Republic) was a phenomenon as frequently associated with a political as with a literary career. Alain-Fournier (1886–1914), Jules Romains (1885–1972), and Marcel Pagnol (1895–1974) were all *fils d'instituteur*. So, too, are three leading French politicians: François Mitterrand's first prime minister, Pierre Mauroy; the left-wing député and present minister of the interior, Jean-Pierre Chevènement; and the socialist whom Jacques Chirac found himself obliged to appoint as Prime Minister in 1997, Lionel Jospin. Jacques Chirac is the grandson, on both his father's and his mother's side, of two men who had also followed this first step out of the manual working class by becoming primary school teachers.

On September 24, 1910, Léon Pompidou married Marie-Louise Chavagnac, one of his colleagues working in the same school at Murat, chef lieu du département du Cantal, in the Auvergne. His wife came from the small village of Montboudif, to which the nearest town is the almost equally unknown La Bourboule, on the way between Clermont-Ferrand and Brive La Gaillarde, in the Département du Cantal, in the south-west of France. It was there that Georges Pompidou was born on July 5, 1911, and it is said that de Gaulle, on first being introduced to the man who would later serve as prime minister for a longer continuous period than any other politician so far in the history of France, intoned the words 'Georges Pompidou, originaire de Montboudif' with the same awed and slightly amused amazement with which a Londoner would greet Albert Hebblethwaite, from Washingborough, Lincolnshire, or a New Yorker a compatriot rejoicing in the name of Hiram J. Rockmetteller, from Great Neck, Arkansas.

Léon Pompidou was an ambitious man who would have liked to continue his education to the point where he sat for the competitive examination known as the *Agrégation*. All French teachers in the public system are civil servants, with their rank, working conditions and salary decided by the state. *Un agrégé*, or *une agrégée*, works shorter hours than a less highly qualified teacher, is paid a higher salary, and is regarded as belonging to the cream of the teaching profession. It was only Léon Pompidou's poor health, coupled with the fact that his wife was frequently ill, which prevented him from achieving his ambition of becoming *un agrégé*. In June 1934, however, his son Georges did it for him, being *reçu premier à l'Agrégation des lettres*.

There were other aspects to Georges Pompidou's career which gave him the right to claim to be even more quintessentially and honourably French than 'le vainqueur de Verdun'. Not only did he have the almost magical appellation of 'fils d'instituteur et d'institutrice', a description which, when applied to me by one of my referees when I was seeking appointment as *lecteur d'anglais* at the Sorbonne in 1953, sent me straight to the top of the list of applicants. He was also *un boursier*, a scholarship boy, who moved, at the age of 19, from the lycée d'Albi to the much more prestigious lycée Louis Le Grand, in Paris.

He did so in accordance with a very French pattern of movement from the provinces to Paris which has provided the subject for novels from Balzac onwards, in order to prepare more effectively than he would have been able to do in Albi for the competition to enter the École Normale Supérieure, the acknowledged gateway to success in the French educational establishment. His fellow students at Louis le Grand included the Senegalese poet and a future President of La République du Sénégal, Léopold Sedar Senghor (1906–), who became a life-long friend; as well as a future French ambassador to the Vatican, René Brouillet, who was later to play a crucial part in enabling him to enter politics.

Politically, Pompidou was then a man of the left. His father had been a committed socialist, and Pompidou read *Le Populaire*, the newspaper of the Section Française de l'Internationale Ouvrière. He joined the Ligue d'action républicaine et socialiste, an anti-fascist organisation created by the man who was to become one of the most successful Présidents du Conseil in the Fourth Republic, Pierre Mendès France (1907–82), and was not afraid to go out into the Latin quarter to do a little street fighting against the royalist grouping known as 'les Camelots du roi'. There is no record of his indulging in fisticuffs with the young François Mitterrand, but the possibility certainly existed. Mitterrand was, at the time, quite an active and enthusiastic supporter of a right-wing organisation, 'les Croix-de-Feu'.

In 1932, Pompidou succeeded in his second attempt at the competitive examination to enter the École Normale Supérieure de la rue d'Ulm. Before the establishment of the École Nationale d'Administration in 1945, this was the acknowledged gateway for anyone wishing to rise to the top in French society, and who did not have the scientific background required by Polytechnique, Ponts et Chaussées, or comparably prestigious Grandes Écoles such as L'École des Mines, or L'École Centrale des Arts et Métiers. The intellectual alertness fostered by the study of literature at the École Normale Supérieure, coupled with the additional courses which he followed at the École Libre des Sciences Politiques, gave Pompidou a set of transferable skills which enabled him not only to follow a wide variety of careers but also to combine them with one another. He had an extraordinary facility for absorbing and analysing knowledge, as well as a misleadingly laid-back attitude. At the written examination for the *Agrégation* in 1934, he handed in his paper an hour before the examination was due to finish, and still came first.

Military service in one form or another has existed in France since 1792, and since the beginning of the nineteenth century there have been few possibilities for exemption. Even literary men, as George Orwell put it, 'knew the weight of a pack', and Jean-Paul Sartre, who also went to the École Normale Supérieure, shortly before Pompidou, and came first in the *Agrégation de philosophie* in 1929, had to spend a year in the army, although he could see out of only one eye. Pompidou did not enjoy his military service. But unlike Sartre, he did take it seriously enough to qualify for a commission, becoming a sous-lieutenant in 1934.

L'École Normale Supérieure de la rue d'Ulm offers its pupils residence as well as education. In this respect, it is rather like a college at Oxford or Cambridge, except for the fact that its pupils must commit themselves in return to serve the state for at least five years. Anyone taking the *Agrégation* is competing to enter into the state sector, and this has drawbacks as well as advantages. A teacher is appointed (*nommé(e)*) at a school where someone with her or his academic speciality is needed. They must go where they are sent, and on completing his military service, Pompidou was appointed in 1935 as teacher of Latin, Greek and French at the lycée Saint-Charles in Marseilles. On October 29, 1935, he married Claude Cahour, the daughter of a senior hospital doctor, and member of a highly respectable upper-middle-class family from Brittany. Socially, it was less of a step upwards than it would have been in the England of the time for a schoolmaster to marry the daughter of a consultant. In France, an *agrégé* is seen as at least the social equal of a doctor, if not his intellectual superior. She proved an excellent wife, sharing his literary tastes, introducing him to the modern, non-figurative painters whose work he was later to use to decorate the walls of the Élysée Palace, and showing herself to be a very good hostess. No children were born to the marriage, but in 1942, they adopted a son, Alain. He later qualified as a doctor, specialised in medical biology, and in 1987 became a leading researcher into the AIDS virus.

In September 1938, Pompidou was appointed to the staff at the lycée de Versailles, and also asked to give classes at the lycée Henri IV, the main Parisian rival to his old school of Louis-le-Grand. Mobilised in 1939, he was released from the army in 1940 and went back to teach at Henri IV, where he employed his leisure hours preparing an edition of Racine's 1669 tragedy, *Britannicus*. He never made any pretence of being involved in the resistance movement, although his widow, Claude Pompidou, in her 1997 autobiography, *L'Élan du coeur*, reported him as having served as a 'letter box' for messages between some of its members.[2] He also discouraged his pupils from criticising 'le maréchal Pétain', whose portrait stood in his classroom, and the low profile which he kept during the occupation did not always endear him to other members of the Gaullist movement.

The decisive moment in what had, up to that point, been a highly successful but also very orthodox career, took place when Georges Pompidou was present as a spectator at the triumphant progress which de Gaulle made along the Champs Élysées on August 15, 1944. The event made such an impression on him that he immediately wrote to one of his friends from École Normale Supérieure, René Trotobas, to ask him if there was any way in which he could enter de Gaulle's service. Trotobas, who later became an ambassador, advised him to make contact with another former friend, René Brouillet, whom they had both known at the lycée Louis-le-Grand, and who was at the time de Gaulle's *directeur de cabinet* (head of his private office).

All societies have their old boy network, and there are a number of advantages for any society in the highly competitive educational system which had brought Georges Pompidou from the obscure village of Montboudif to the position where he was an established and highly qualified teacher at one of the most highly regarded schools in Paris. It provides a way whereby men and women of talent are easily recognised as available and qualified to serve their fellow citizens. Pompidou's career had always been an illustration of the Napoleonic ideal of 'la carrière ouverte aux talents'. The need which France had of such talents, in the aftermath of the turmoil created by the experience of war, occupation and resistance, offered him the opportunity he was seeking to serve his country. At the same time, and perhaps even more importantly, it gave his country the chance of using his abilities.

De Gaulle's career, as I have argued, underlines a particular feature of French political culture. It illustrates, like that of the two Napoleons, and that of Philippe Pétain, with what relative ease a military man could take over in France when the normal political system had broken down. Pompidou's career, as *un fils d'instituteur et d'institutrice* who rises to become president of the Republic, may well constitute an event which is as rare in practice as the 'from log cabin to White House' syndrome is in the United States. But if it does illustrate a myth, it is one which is as intensely French, and which is a good deal more encouraging, than the portrait displayed in 1940 of Marshal Pétain.

1946–58

Although Pompidou himself denied the legend that de Gaulle is supposed to have asked someone to find him 'un agrégé sachant écrire',[3] it is a good story. It reflects the importance which de Gaulle himself, like his fellow countrymen, attached to language, and helps to explain why Pompidou was able to rise so quickly in his service. This was not, if Pompidou is to be believed, because his handwriting was either particularly elegant or especially legible. When he wrote to de Gaulle, on January 3, 1969, to voice his complaints of how he had recently been treated by some of his fellow Gaullists, he began by explaining that he was sending him a typed letter 'pour vous éviter la peine de déchiffrer mon illegible écriture' (to save you the trouble of deciphering my illegible handwriting).[4] What made Pompidou so valuable a collaborator was his ability to express himself clearly. Of all the transferable skills which he perfected at the lycée Louis-le Grand and the École Normale Supérieure, this was undoubtedly the most valuable.

Georges Pompidou had been a civil servant, a member of the corps de l'Éducation Nationale, since his entry into the teaching profession in 1935. In the autumn of 1946, de Gaulle arranged for him to become a different kind of public servant by having him appointed to the Conseil d'État, the court of appeal for administrative law. In spite of having no previous experience of the law, Pompidou was immediately at home, just as he was as a lecturer at the Institut d'Études politiques, a post which he held at the same time as he was a member of the Conseil d'État, and worked in a semi-private capacity for de Gaulle.

In early 1946, Pompidou also became treasurer of the Fondation Anne de Gaulle, the series of homes for handicapped children established for children suffering from Down's syndrome and other inherited disabilities, and financed by the royalties from de Gaulle's books. He showed great skill and tact in dealing with all the practical problems, winning the esteem and friendship of Yvonne de Gaulle, and strengthening his position as de Gaulle's éminence grise. Here again, it was a job which he combined with his duties as a member of the Conseil d'État, much as a British civil servant might work in the evenings for a charitable organisation.

What is slightly more surprising, to the English-speaking observer accustomed to a stricter concept of political neutrality in the civil service, is that there seems to have been no objection to Georges Pompidou, as a member of the Conseil d'État, one of what are known as Les Grands Corps de l'État, also working for de Gaulle, as he did from April 23, 1948 onwards, as his *chef de cabinet*. Theoretically, this was a private appointment, and Pompidou never became a card carrying member of the Rassemblement du Peuple Français (RPF). But from the moment that he had formed the RPF, on April 7, 1947, de Gaulle had become a political figure with a very definite political agenda: that of changing the Constitution of the Fourth Republic and setting up a different régime in its place.

However, the French have a more flexible concept than the one which exists either in the United States or in the United Kingdom of how the idea of a politically neutral civil service should be translated into practice. In Whitehall or in Washington, the idea of a senior civil servant working more or less openly for a political figure while still continuing to receive his salary from the tax-payer would cause more than the occasional raised eyebrow. She or he would be expected to resign, and asked to do so if they did not go of their own accord. It is less strange in the political culture of France. There, movement between the civil service and the world of politics, as indeed between the higher civil service and the world of business, is much more common than it is in the English-speaking democracies.

This is made possible by the possibility for any civil servant to obtain either *une mise en détachement* or *une mise en disponibilité*, a term best translated as unpaid leave.[5] In the case of the former, she or he goes to work in another part of the civil service, receiving the same automatic promotion, and retaining the same pension rights, as they would in their *corps d'origine*. In the second, the civil servant leaves her or his *corps* on a temporary basis in order to pursue a career elsewhere, generally in politics, but can always go back to the civil service if the political career envisaged proves unsatisfactory.

Members of Les Grands Corps de l'État are traditionally granted a fair degree of latitude in the way they fulfil their duties. It is partly this long-established custom which enabled Georges Pompidou to combine being a *maître des requêtes* (roughly the equivalent in rank to a deputy secretary, the third down from the top in the British civil service, just below a permanent under secretary) in the Conseil d'État, with lecturing at the École des Sciences Politiques, while at the same time working for de Gaulle.

Pompidou was clearly very good with money. He managed the finances of the RPF as well as those of the Fondation Anne de Gaulle, and when de Gaulle dissolved the movement, on May 6, 1953, began to look about for another appointment, outside the public service. On February 1, 1954, he was offered a post with the Rothschild banking group, and he remained with them until de Gaulle's return to power in 1958. He then, on June 1, resumed the post of *chef de cabinet* which he had had in the days of the RPF. Claude Pompidou, who resembled Yvonne de Gaulle in not wishing her husband to follow a political career, insisted in the first instance on his obtaining leave of absence from the bank for only six months. Pompidou consequently returned to the Rothschild group in January 1959, where he remained until de Gaulle appointed him prime minister on April 3, 1962.

By 1953, Pompidou had thus been one of de Gaulle's closest collaborators for over seven years. In addition to his work for la Fondation Anne de Gaulle, he had also negotiated the publication of the three volumes of de Gaulle's *Mémoires de Guerre*: *L'Appel*, *L'Unité* and *Le Salut*, with the publishing house of Plon. Their appearance in October 1954, over a year after de Gaulle had dissolved the Rassemblement du Peuple Français, performed the useful function of keeping him in the public eye, and over 100,000 copies were sold in the first month. Although he had played no part in the events which had enabled de Gaulle to come back to power in 1958, it was Pompidou and Pompidou alone who accompanied de Gaulle to the Élysée Palace on January 8, 1959 for the official ceremony in which René Coty handed over the presidency of the Republic.

The close collaboration between de Gaulle and Pompidou had obvious advantages for both men. De Gaulle knew that he was a difficult man to get on with. Pompidou, in contrast, was the perfect go-between, expert in soothing people down, brilliant at finding compromises acceptable to all parties. One of the most urgent problems which de Gaulle had to face, even before he tackled the question of Algeria, was the state of the nation's finances. The presence of Antoine Pinay as minister of finance in the government which Michel Debré formed on January 9, 1959 was a guarantee to *la France profonde* that there would be some prudent house-keeping. But de Gaulle did not like Pinay, and the feeling was mutual.

In his eyes, Pinay represented the France which had accepted Marshal Pétain. He had not been among the 80 députés et sénateurs who had voted against giving full powers to Pétain on July 10, 1940. He was also an enthusiastic supporter of closer ties between France and the United States, and in favour of L'Algérie Française. Pinay, in turn, suspected de Gaulle of being a military adventurer, and disliked his obvious intention to reduce the importance of parliament. But the two men had to get on together, at least in public, if confidence in de Gaulle's economic policy was to be maintained, and this was something which Pompidou achieved.

He had, thanks to his experience with the Rothschild group, essentially the outlook of a merchant banker. This made him an expansionist in economic matters, and it was due to his influence that the new franc launched on January 1, 1959, in which one nouveau franc replaced 100 anciens francs, was also accompanied by a devaluation of 19.5 per cent. This gave French industry an immediate competitive advantage in the export markets, but one which boosted the economy at the risk of causing inflation. This was not a danger which particularly worried Pompidou, and one of the purely technical reasons for regretting his early death, in April 1974, was that it prevented his admirers from seeing how he would have dealt with the great inflation of the 1970s and early 1980s.

Pompidou also played a major role, in collaboration with Michel Debré, in elaborating the system for electing members of the Assemblée Nationale adopted by the Fifth Republic, that of the *scrutin majoritaire uninominal à deux tours* (single member constituency, two ballot election). In this, only a candidate polling over 50 per cent of the votes cast is elected in the first round, and any candidate scoring less than 12.5 per cent is automatically precluded from standing in the second ballot. The equivalent of the British 'first past the post' (*scrutin uninominal à un tour*) system operates only in the second round, which takes place a week later. The decision as to which of the candidates who have scored more than 12.5 per cent are going to stand in this second ballot comes after a series of negotiations intended to ensure that less favoured candidate or candidates of the right will stand down in order to leave only one conservative contender, while the same process takes place on the left.

Although the *scrutin uninominal à deux tours* has been a crucial factor in the relative bipolarisation of French political life since 1958, it has not always avoided the situation where the party winning a majority of seats in parliament does so after receiving less than half the votes cast. In June 1968, when the Gaullist Union des Démocrates pour la Cinquième République (UD-Ve Rép.) won a comfortable majority of 294 seats in an Assemblée Nationale of 485, it had only

46.39 per cent of the votes cast in the second ballot. Even in 1981, when the Socialist Party ended up with an absolute majority of 269 seats in an Assemblée Nationale of 491 members, it did so on the strength of 49.28 per cent of the votes cast in the second ballot for the alliance which it had formed with the much smaller Mouvement des Radicaux de Gauche (MRG).

It was not until the second round of the parliamentary elections of May–June 1997 imprudently called by Jacques Chirac that a group of parties winning a majority in the Assemblée Nationale also received half the votes cast in the second ballot. The left's majority of 319 seats in parliament over 245 for the right corresponded to 53.07 per cent of the votes cast for Lionel Jospin's party and its allies, conveniently known as 'la gauche plurielle'. The combined forces of the Rassemblement pour la République and the Union pour la Démocratie Française received 46.04 per cent.[6]

The *scrutin uninominal à deux tours* gives a great advantage to candidates from any party who can persuade potential rivals who share its general outlook to stand down in its favour at the second ballot. This creates an in-built disadvantage for any party which, like the National Front, has a set of views which preclude alliances, and it has been one of the factors which has brought the socialists and the communists closer together. It also helps to explain why, since 1978, there have been two main right-wing parties, the Rassemblement pour la République created by Jacques Chirac on December 5, 1976, and the Union pour la Démocratie Française, established on February 1, 1978 by Valéry Giscard d'Estaing. Pompidou, like all Gaullists, liked the system because it did tend, for all its potential unfairness, to produce a government with a solid majority. The similarity with the British system, in which no government since the National Government of 1930 has actually had more than half the electorate voting for it, is in this respect not entirely a drawback.

On February 14, 1961 Pompidou was the main negotiator involved in the first attempt by the French government to enter into some kind of negotiation with the Algerian Front de Libération Nationale. Although he had kept his promise to Claude Pompidou and gone back to working for Rothschild early in 1959, after the six months which he had promised de Gaulle as his *chef de cabinet*, he nevertheless agreed to lead the French delegation which met the FLN delegates at Lucerne. It was this meeting which led, on March 30, 1961, to the announcement that further negotiations were to take place at Évian. Although it was Louis Joxe, an early supporter of de Gaulle, who had been secretary of the Comité national de libération in 1943, who led the final negotiations, Pompidou continued to play an important role. As the private adviser in whom de Gaulle seems to have had more confidence than in any member of his government, it was he who insisted, at the time of the attempted military putsch in Algeria in 1961, that de Gaulle should make the crucial speech on radio and television on April 23 which saved the situation.

1962–8

Once de Gaulle had carried through his policy of giving Algeria its independence, he had no more use for Michel Debré. Pompidou, who had the great advantage of not belonging to any political party, consequently offered the possibility of a new start. As soon as he could be persuaded to leave the Rothschild bank, and although he had not yet stood for any elected office, he was appointed prime minister on April 14, 1962.

This became, in retrospect, the beginning of a pattern that was to recur under each of de Gaulle's successors as president. It is one whereby the president, whom Article 8 of the 1958 Constitution gives the right of appointing his prime minister (*il nomme le Premier Ministre*), begins by choosing the person he has to, before going on to appoint the person he prefers. Pompidou himself did it on June 23, 1972, when he replaced Jacques Chaban-Delmas by Pierre Messmer, Giscard d'Estaing did it on August 27, 1976, when he appointed Raymond Barre after the departure of Jacques Chirac, François Mitterrand on July 1984 when he replaced Pierre Mauroy by Laurent Fabius, and again on May 15, 1991 when he appointed Édith Cresson in the place of Michel Rocard. Only Jacques Chirac, who had to abandon Alain Juppé between the first and second rounds of the legislative elections of June 1997, and then appoint the socialist Lionel Jospin, whose party had won the elections, on June 1, has so far been an exception.

Pompidou also had the great advantage of having exactly the same conception of the prime minister's role as de Gaulle did. This was that the president took the major decisions, which the prime minister carried out. Although Pompidou was, as he showed when he became president in May 1969, not at all happy about de Gaulle's two vetoes, on January 1963 and again in May 1967, on British entry into the European Economic Community, he made no public protest. The positively filial devotion which he showed towards de Gaulle, and which occasionally led to speculation as to how satisfying his emotional relationship had been with Léon Pompidou, began to break down only with the events of May 1968.

The events which shook France in May 1968 began at a new university at Nanterre, in the suburbs of Paris, whose buildings had been put up in a particularly unattractive semi-industrial landscape with no consideration for the social needs of the students. There was also a degree of overcrowding which was unusually high even in French universities, and which stems from the fact that anyone with the baccalauréat can register as a university student. A large number of both undergraduate and postgraduate students at Nanterre were taking sociology, and thus had little possibility of ever finding employment. This led to the feeling on their part that this was the fault of society, and especially of what they saw as the essentially conservative form given to it by the French middle class and sustained by de Gaulle.

The associated problems of overcrowding and a high failure rate existed in almost as acute a form in Paris itself. There, too, the overcrowding was such that nobody disbelieved the story that the only way of ensuring a place in the biology lecture for first-year medical students which began in one of the main amphitheatres of the Sorbonne at ten in the morning, was to go and sit through the lecture on Egyptian archaeology which started in the same amphitheatre at nine. There was also the same excess of supply over demand in students of Arts, and in what it was becoming fashionable to describe as Social Sciences, as there was in Nanterre.

The movement had begun in Nanterre in March 1966 as a result of an incident during the visit of François Missoffe, the minister for youth and sport. He had gone to open the swimming pool in one of the few student residences to have been put up at Nanterre, and was interrupted in his speech by a student in sociology, Daniel Cohn-Bendit, who told him that the book he had recently published on the problems encountered by young people in the world of the 1960s was a load of rubbish. In particular, said Cohn-Bendit, Missoffe had made no mention of sex.

His criticism was immediately understood by the audience as a reference to the fact that it was, at the time, forbidden for boys to enter the part of the student residence where the girls lived, and vice versa. The minister made no reference to this, but tried instead to get the audience on his side by making a reference to Cohn-Bendit's appearance. 'Looking like you do' he said ('Avec la tête que vous avez'), 'I'm not surprised that you have problems with the opposite sex'. Cohn-Bendit had red hair and freckles, together with a somewhat pugnacious appearance. There was an immediate outcry, which by March 22 had become a protest movement which led to what soon became known in England as a 'sit-in' of the administrative buildings. On May 2, the protests had spread to Paris. On May 3, all lectures were cancelled at the Sorbonne, and the buildings closed.

The slowness with which both Pompidou and de Gaulle understood what was happening can be judged from the fact that on May 2, Pompidou went on an official visit to Afghanistan, and on May 14 de Gaulle left for a state visit to Rumania. By the time Pompidou came back on May 11, the situation was getting increasingly out of hand. Throughout the night of May 6, some 20,000 students had come out on to the streets to protest against the earlier arrest and imprisonment of other student demonstrators, and the police themselves gave the figure of 600 wounded in the riots. On the night of May 10, barricades went up throughout the Latin quarter, and although Pompidou's decision, on his return from Afghanistan, to re-open the Sorbonne, avoided more immediate bloodshed, it did not end the crisis. As soon as the police left, the students re-occupied the university buildings, and held long meetings to discuss their problems and decide what to do next.

There was a sharp difference between de Gaulle and Pompidou as to how the authorities should proceed. De Gaulle wanted the police to intervene to evacuate the Sorbonne, and proposed to forbid a march planned to take place on May 13 from Denfert-Rochereau, about three miles to the south of the Sorbonne, to the Latin quarter. Pompidou, conscious of the violence and possible loss of life which would almost certainly be caused by an attempt to stop a march likely to be joined by some 200,000 demonstrators, while at the same time forcing the students out of the Sorbonne, took a more moderate attitude, allowing the students to remain in the Sorbonne and the march to take place. It proved to be the right thing to do, and de Gaulle took off for Rumania on May 14 from a France in which a new civil war had been averted.

On the evening of May 14, Pompidou had to confront, as prime minister, a tumultuous debate in the Assemblée Nationale. In de Gaulle's absence he was visibly in charge, and replied in one of his best speeches to François Mitterrand's demand that the government should immediately resign. He did not make the mistake of condemning the students. It was not, he pointed out, the sons and daughters of the working class who were leading the movement, or who were even involved in it. What he called, in remembrance of his own family background, 'la jeunesse ouvrière et paysanne qui connaît le prix du pain et la dure nécessité de l'effort' (the young people of the working class and peasantry who know what a loaf of bread costs and how hard you have to work) had so far not been involved, and his remark remains a useful reminder of what was to happen elsewhere. The movement which immediately became known as 'May 68' remained essentially a middle-class phenomenon, a fact which led sociologists who followed the lead of Herbert Marcuse (1898–1979) to argue that it was students who had now become the revolutionary élite which would overthrow bourgeois society.

This was not an event which Georges Pompidou wished to see taking place, but he did see why the French students were so unhappy. It was, he argued in his speech to the National Assembly on May 14, 1968, often the best and most sensitive among them who were affected by the breakdown of traditional society and the disappearance of its values. While ensuring that order was maintained, the government was trying to understand what was happening, and to find a solution to the problems which had caused what looked increasingly like a general uprising. It was a generous diagnosis, which had the advantage of showing a readiness to negotiate which looked forward to the peaceful ending of the crisis a few weeks later.

Before this happened, however, the situation rapidly became worse. On May 15, the workers spontaneously occupied the Renault car factories in the Paris area, and on May 20 a more general strike began which spread to other sectors of French industry. It was not a move encouraged by the Communist Party, which maintained throughout that France did not face a revolutionary situation of the classical Marxist type ('la situation n'est pas révolutionnaire' was their way of putting it), and was annoyed to see control of the organised working class slipping out of its hands. On his return from Rumania on May 18, de Gaulle gave one his more aggressive and less successful speeches, proclaiming 'la réforme oui; la chienlit, non' (reforms, yes; fouling your own nest, no), and announcing a reform on one of his favourite ideas, 'la participation'.

Gaullism, as a political doctrine, had always had a vaguely left-wing appeal as well as a populist and nationalistic one. But it was never clear quite what de Gaulle meant by the term. Pompidou told him that he would be quite happy to see how 'la participation' could be made to work if only he could be told what it was. As far as he was concerned, he added, it meant either the sovietisation of factories, or the introduction into them of the *régime d'assemblée* of the Third and Fourth republics. It was, in addition, impossible to see what question might be asked in a referendum.

Unlike Pompidou, who had enjoyed a highly successful career as a merchant banker, de Gaulle had never had any practical experience of the commercial or industrial world, and the disagreement about 'la participation' was one of several incidents which made the events of May 1968 the beginning of the end for de Gaulle himself and for his relationship with Georges Pompidou. The event which made Pompidou increasingly conscious of the possibility that de Gaulle's best work for France was now behind him took place on May 29. Suddenly, without warning, de Gaulle disappeared, reappearing in an equally unexpected manner at the French military base at Baden Baden.

He had not, according to General Massu's account, gone to see him in order to find out whether the army would be prepared to intervene to restore order. It was, again according to Massu, because he was going through a period of intense depression, and felt that there was nobody he could turn to but an old army acquaintance.[7] Whatever Massu told him, de Gaulle certainly returned to Paris in a different frame of mind, albeit without being quite conscious of how deeply wounded Pompidou felt at being left, as prime minister, without the slightest news of what the head of state was doing.

De Gaulle's subsequent announcement, on May 30, that he was dissolving the Assemblée Nationale, led to one of Pompidou's greatest triumphs: the winning of the subsequent legislative elections, on June 23 and 30, 1968, by a wider margin of seats and a higher proportion of votes on the second ballot than had ever been achieved in any French parliamentary election. With 294 seats out of a total of 485, the newly formed Union pour la Défense de la République (UDR) had an absolute majority which replaced the situation created by the elections held only the previous year, on March 5 and March 12, 1967. This had produced a National Assembly in which the traditional Gaullist party (L'Union pour la République) UDR, in alliance with the more left-wing Gaullist Union démocratique du travail (UDT), with only 177 seats, had been dependent for its majority on Valéry Giscard d'Estaing's forty-three Républicains Indépendants.

It was a victory which underlined the support which the parliamentary democracy of the Fifth Republic enjoyed over the attempt to overthrow what the more politically conscious activists of May 68 called the 'bourgeois state'. It was, certainly, a vindication of the Communist Party's view that the situation created by the Parisian students had no long-term revolutionary potential. But it was also very much Georges Pompidou's own work, a reflection of the appeal which his personality and values had for *la France profonde*, as well as tribute to the skill which he had shown in the negotiations which effectively put an end to the crisis.

These began on May 25, and led eventually not only to a general return to work but, more importantly, to the re-opening of the petrol pumps which had been closed during the strike which had begun on May 15. The French, and more particularly the Parisians, could now go on their traditional Whitsun holidays, and their anxiety to do so showed how popular the consumer society had become in France. However much the politically conscious students might denounce it, the economic prosperity which the policies adopted by Georges Pompidou had always encouraged was something which everybody wanted. There was, of course, a price to pay for the wage increases of between 10 per cent and 15 per cent which Pompidou negotiated with the trade unions, and which deprived the student rebels of the working-class support which they rightly saw as essential to any serious attempt to take over the state.

It was a price which was paid on August 20, 1969, two months after Pompidou's election as president of the Republic, and took the form of a sudden devaluation of the franc by 12.5 per cent. The wage increases granted by the accords de Grenelle had led to an increase in the production costs of French industry, and to a consequent increase in the price of French goods intended for export. The only way in which they could become competitive again was by a devaluation of the franc, and it was Pompidou's own decision to do this. Whereas de Gaulle had set his face against devaluation in the aftermath of May 68, and tried to protect the value of the franc by the introduction on November 25, 1968 of rigorous exchange controls, Pompidou adopted the less authoritarian and more rational attitude of accepting the law of supply and demand. If the markets would not buy francs at the price fixed by the French state, the only solution lay in bringing the price down to the level at which they would.

The aims of the student rebels of 1968 had been less clearly formulated than those of the *pieds noirs*. There was nothing unreasonable about the desire of the European Algerians to stay in the country in which they had always lived. The slogans which decorated the walls of Paris in May 1968 had a certain poetic charm to them. It is nevertheless hard to see precisely how the application of 'L'imagination au pouvoir', or 'On fera la révolution. Après, on verra' (Imagination in power, or We'll have a revolution. Then we'll see) could produce a society in which trains ran, schools stayed open, and grandma got the French equivalent of her nourishing milk stout. In the event, the student rebellion of 1968 did not even manage to improve the French university system. This still remains characterised by the same overcrowding, the same shortage of facilities, and the same high failure rate as in the 1960s.

It was Pompidou's shrewd grasp of how his fellow-countrymen were likely to behave which led him, in May 1968, to do everything he could to reduce the number and violence of possible confrontations. Had he not given the order to re-open the Sorbonne on May 13, and allowed the march from Denfert-Rochereau to take place, the clash between police and demonstrators would have given rise to serious bloodshed. He did not succeed completely. The French police have never heard of the concept of minimum response. At least two people were killed, and over 1,000 badly enough injured to need hospital treatment. But had de Gaulle been in charge alone, or with a less intelligent prime minister, the situation could well have degenerated into one of open civil war.

This was the danger that Georges Pompidou played a major part in avoiding, but he received little thanks for his pains. On July 21, 1968, he was replaced as prime minister by Maurice Couve de Murville, a career diplomat who had been foreign minister ever since de Gaulle's return to power in 1968. He had also, unlike Pompidou, been at de Gaulle's side during the second world war, as secretary general of the Gouvernement Provisoire de la République Française in Algiers in 1943, and his appointment was widely seen as a deliberate snub to Pompidou and a reminder of the fact that de Gaulle possessed a right to govern France which did not depend upon electoral victories of the type which Pompidou had just pulled off on June 23 and June 30.

This was not an entirely fair impression, since Pompidou had apparently told de Gaulle in June 1968 that he wished to be relieved of his responsibilities as prime minister.[8] The manner of his going nevertheless reinforced the impression that de Gaulle had a genius for ingratitude, and one of the implications of the announcement that Pompidou had been 'placé en réserve de la République' was that he was always there to be called on, as well as to be dismissed, whenever de Gaulle chose. In so far as Pompidou had no independent power base, this was true. It was only on March 5, 1967, after more than twenty years as de Gaulle's most influential councillor and executive, that he was elected to parliament. In the first round of the legislative elections, he became député du Cantal, the Département in which Montboudif is situated.

If one excepts his earlier election, in March 1965, to the relatively minor responsibilities of a conseiller municipal for the small town of Carjac, in the Département du Lot, it was the first time that Pompidou had had to face the electorate. He certainly did better in 1967 than

Couve de Murville had done. The elections of March 12 and March 19 of that year had not been a success for the Gaullist party, then known as the Union pour la Nouvelle République (UNR). After doing reasonably well in the first round, the UNR had seen the left do much better than expected in the second. This was largely because the alliance between socialists and communists had worked well enough to make the system of *désistements*, whereby the less-favoured candidate in a constituency stands down to give one of his allies a better chance, worked well in their favour. In addition to leaving the UNR dependent for its parliamentary survival on Valéry Giscard d'Estaing's Républicains Indépendants, the second round of the March 1967 elections had seen four of de Gaulle's ministers lose their seats.

Couve de Murville had lost in what would normally have been a safe Gaullist seat in the seventh arrondissement of Paris, being defeated by the old parliamentary hand, Édouard Frédéric-Dupont. De Gaulle had thus not been able to carry out what had apparently been his intention of making him prime minister in 1967 and had to soldier on with Pompidou. This was, as it turned out, a very good thing, since it is impossible to imagine Couve de Murville dealing as intelligently as Pompidou did with the events of May 1968.[9]

Like Pompidou's career between 1946 and 1968, Couve de Murville's role as de Gaulle's foreign minister is a reminder of a similarity between the practices of the Fifth French Republic and what happens in the United States. Thus, without having been elected to any representative office, Henry Kissinger (1923–) virtually ran American foreign policy between 1968 and 1976, only to be relieved of his responsibilities with the election of President Carter and the rise of the equally unelected – and, like Kissinger, foreign born – Zbigniew Brzezinski (1928–).

While it would be difficult to imagine de Gaulle entrusting the management of French foreign policy or national security to a man born in Germany or Poland, it was this type of relationship between the president and his advisers and executives that he clearly regarded as ideal. While he quite liked his ministers to acquire an aura of democratic respectability by being elected to a seat as député, this was by no means essential. They would, in any case, have to hand over their seat to their *suppléant* on taking up ministerial office. Once this had been done, and their duty to the government rather than to parliament reasserted, they were his men.

1968–74

It may well be, in this respect, that the main reason for the appointment as prime minister of Couve de Murville on July 21, 1968 was that
de Gaulle felt that Pompidou was getting too big for his boots. De
Gaulle paid a great compliment to Claude Pompidou when the couple
came to dinner at the Élysée on June 25. 'Madame, je puis vous dire
que votre mari a tenu',[10] is the nearest one can get in French to 'your
husband played a good defensive innings'. But he was aware that
Pompidou had not been there in the great procession along the
Champs Élysées which Charles Pasqua had organised to show support
for de Gaulle on May 30, 1968, and which is said to have brought a
million people out on to the streets of Paris.[11]

De Gaulle's behaviour had always been like that of the man who, in
Alexander Pope's *Epistle to Dr Arbuthnot*, 'bears, like the Turk, no
brother near the throne'.

Pompidou had perhaps made the mistake, for the first time in their
long relationship, of suggesting that he knew how indispensable he had
become, and de Gaulle's behaviour in November 1968 suggests a petti-
ness of mind which recalls Talleyrand's comment after one of his less
amicable interviews with Napoleon I: 'Quel dommage qu'un si grand
homme ait été si mal élevé' (What a pity that so great a man should
have been so badly brought up).

De Gaulle also did nothing when the rumours began to spread, in
November 1968, that Claude Pompidou, whom he had known for over
twenty years, had not only been taking part in a series of sexual orgies
– the French term of 'parties fines' is misleadingly euphemistic – but
had allowed herself to be photographed. With the power and influence
at his disposal, he could have put an end to these rumours in a day by
the simple device of letting it be known that he and Madame de
Gaulle had invited the Pompidous, and the Pompidous alone, to a
private dinner party. Madame de Gaulle was the epitome of French
provincial Catholic bourgeois respectability. Pierre Viansson-Ponté
noted in 1963 how she

> pitilessly removed from the General's social circle any man or
> woman who had been divorced, felt no hesitation in striking off
> the list of people to be invited to a private party any couple who

had had merely a civil marriage, and cut dead anyone who was suspected of leading an irregular sexual life.[12]

As it was, the de Gaulles did nothing, and the events supposedly linking the Pompidous with the discovery of the murdered body of Stephan Marcovitch, one of the actor Alain Delon's bodyguards, continued for several months to be the centre of gossip about them in smart Parisian circles.[13] The rumours were certainly spread, and may well have been invented, by traditional Gaullists who had never liked Pompidou, and wanted to do everything they could to spoil his chances of being elected president after de Gaulle had left office.

Although de Gaulle seems to have had no gift for friendship, Pompidou was not a man to bear grudges, and campaigned vigorously for a 'yes' vote of April 27, 1969 on regionalisation and the reform of the Senate. But he had, by the efficiency with which he had dealt with the events of May 68, shown that he was somebody who could take over if de Gaulle was defeated and carried out his threat to resign. It was no longer possible, as it had been in the referenda of September 28, 1958, January 8, 1961 or November 6, 1962, for de Gaulle to produce what had become the familiar argument of 'Moi ou le chaos'. The solid, dependable, avuncular figure of Georges Pompidou was there, as quintessentially French as de Gaulle or Pétain, and a good deal younger than either.

There is little doubt that Pompidou was caught unawares by the question suddenly put to him by a journalist in Rome who asked him on January 17, 1969 whether he would be a candidate for the presidency at the next election. He replied that he obviously would be, but added that he was in no hurry. His remarks nevertheless annoyed de Gaulle, who made a point of announcing at the next cabinet meeting, on January 22, that he had every intention of staying in power until the next presidential election, which was not due until December 1972. Relations between the two men never recovered, and while de Gaulle assured Pompidou in a private letter that he would be voting for him in the presidential elections of June 1969 brought about by his resignation after the 'no' vote in the referendum of April 27, he gave him no public support.

Pompidou did not really need it. Although he failed, as de Gaulle had done in December 1965, to be elected on the first ballot of the 1969 presidential election, he had little difficulty in defeating the president of the Senate, Alain Poher, in the run-off on June 15, 1969. Although more people voted for opposition candidates on the first ballot, on June 1, there was no chance of an alliance on the left which might have defeated Pompidou. Poher received 5,268,651 votes, the PCF candidate, Jacques Duclos, 4,808,285, the socialist Gaston Defferre 1,333,222, the candidate for the left-wing Parti Socialiste Unifié, Michel Rocard, 881,616, and Alain Krivine, the Trotskyst presenting himself as the representative of 'May 68', 239,106. The fact that Pompidou received 10,051,816 votes out of the total of 22,603,998 nevertheless revealed a breadth and solidity of support which explains his victory over Poher on June 15 by 11,064,371 to 7,943,118, or 58.21 per cent over 41.78 per cent of those voting – a lead of 16.43 per cent.

Although Pompidou thus won by a higher percentage of those voting than any other candidate apart from de Gaulle since the first election of the president by universal suffrage in 1965, the abstentions in the second ballot remain the highest so far recorded: 31.14 per cent. In the second ballot of the December 1965 election, de Gaulle had had a percentage majority of 10.3 per cent over François Mitterrand, with a 15.6 per cent abstention rate. In May 1974, Valéry Giscard d'Estaing had the narrowest victory so far, of 0.33 per cent, against 50.66 per cent over 49.33 per cent for François Mitterrand, with 12.66 per cent of the electorate abstaining. In 1981, Mitterrand had 51.76 per cent over 48.24 per cent for Giscard d'Estaing, with an abstention rate in the second ballot of 13.57 per cent. In 1988, Mitterrand beat Chirac by 54.02 per cent over 45.98 per cent, a lead of 8.04 per cent, with an abstention rate on the second ballot of 15.93 per cent and on May 5, 1995, Jacques Chirac beat Lionel Jospin by 52.64 per cent against 47.36 per cent in the second round, a lead of 5.25 per cent with an abstention rate of 19.49 per cent.

The French system for the election of the president, with its rule that only two candidates can go forward to the second round, has the advantage over the system in force in the United States, where 17 of the 49 presidents so far elected have received less than 50 per cent of the popular vote. Although no candidate for the presidency of the Fifth Republic has yet succeeded in being elected on the first ballot, the French president invariably has the moral advantage of having had more people voting for him than against him in the decisive second round. This does not necessarily make him more powerful than the leader of a political party winning a majority of seats in the Assemblée Nationale. Since the president has no legislative powers, and no authority to raise taxes, he has no choice but to behave as Mitterrand did in 1986 when faced with the right-wing majority produced by the legislative elections of March 16, and appoint a prime minister capable of having laws passed and a budget approved.

This is not something which Georges Pompidou either had to do or could see any president of the Fifth Republic being obliged to do. For him, as for de Gaulle, the Constitution of the Fifth Republic could work properly only if there were a total agreement between the president and the prime minister – or, to put it more directly, only if the prime minister were prepared do what the president told him. This was how both he and Michel Debré had behaved towards de Gaulle, and how he expected his prime ministers to behave towards him. Debré never objected publicly to de Gaulle's abandonment of the policy of L'Algérie Française, and Pompidou had not disagreed openly with de Gaulle's two vetoes, in January 1963 and June 1967, on the British application to join the European Economic Community.

This was, as soon became apparent, an issue on which his views were radically different from those of de Gaulle, and one of the most important events of his presidency was a change in French policy which enabled the United Kingdom to become a member of the EEC on January 1, 1973. But so long as he was de Gaulle's prime minister, Pompidou did what he was told, and he clearly expected his prime ministers to do the same. Article 20 of the 1958 Constitution might say that it was the government which 'decides and conducts the Nation's policy' ('le Gouvernement détermine et conduit la politique de la Nation'), but Article 8 says that the prime minister, who according to Article 21 'directs the action of the government', was appointed by the president. While not explicitly saying that the prime minister is responsible to the president, this was what de Gaulle had always assumed that it meant, and neither as prime minister, nor now as president, did Pompidou disagree.

It was this reading of the Constitution which led, in 1972, to the first occasion in which a prime minister left office because of a disagreement over policy. De Gaulle had always insisted that his prime ministers should, on appointment, sign an undated letter of resignation. This enabled him to implement the second sentence in Article 8 of the Constitution which states that the president 'puts an end to the prime minister's functions on being presented by him with his government's resignation' ('Il met fin à ses fonctions sur la présentation par celui-ci de la démission de son gouvernement'). He was thus in a position where he could assert his presidential prerogative at any time, and did not fail to do so.

Although Pompidou did not follow the same procedure on July 5, 1972, when he secured the resignation of his first prime minister, Jacques Chaban-Delmas, whom he had appointed on June 20, 1969, only five days after being elected president, the result was the same: the re-assertion of presidential over prime ministerial power. Two reasons made the resignation convenient for both men: the first was a question of protocol rather than of policy, and the second an embarrassing issue of personal finance. On September 16, 1969, in his opening speech as prime minister to the Assemblée Nationale, Chaban-Delmas had proclaimed his intention of trying to bring about what he called 'la nouvelle société'. It was, he explained, to be more open and more dynamic, with a less dominant role for the state, and more autonomy for public enterprises such as the Société Nationale des Chemins de Fer Français (the SNCF; nationalised by the Popular Front of 1936), and greater liberty for the Organisation de Radio et de Telévision Française (ORTF), still under strict government control.

These were not ideas to which Pompidou himself was hostile. One of his main aims was to make France a more highly industrialised nation, and Chaban-Demas's suggestion for the setting up of an Institute of Industrial Development was exactly the kind of proposal that he might have made himself. What created problems was the manner in which Chaban-Delmas had put them forward. He had given his speech at three o'clock in the afternoon, and the text of it had not arrived at the Élysée Palace until half-past two. Pompidou's main preoccupation at the time was to ensure that the institutions of the Fifth Republic functioned as smoothly as possible in the period immediately following the departure of its creator. It did not seem to him that this was likely to happen with a prime minister who seemed anxious to usurp the traditional prerogative of the president to take the initiative in important matters of national policy.

Pompidou had been careful, in forming his first government, to ensure the support of 'les gaullistes historiques', the men who had been part of Gaullism in its heroic period of 1940–4. Chaban-Delmas was one of them, having been active in the resistance movement under the name of Chaban before becoming military delegate to the provisional government established by de Gaulle in Algiers in 1943. He had ended the war as général de brigade, was a Compagnon de la Libération, had been active in national politics in the Gaullist interest since the end of the war and mayor of Bordeaux since 1947. He was also an international tennis and rugby player, and had the quality, unusual among Frenchmen even today, of playing to a single figure handicap in golf.

As a man with all the qualities, he was thus an essential ally in Pompidou's quest to ensure that the legitimacy which he had acquired by his electoral successes was echoed by his continued acceptability to the Gaullist élite. Although Pompidou had said, in his press conference on January 21, 1971, that he held this *légitimité* (a key word in French politics; like *la souveraineté*, you either have it or you don't) from his free election by the French people, Pompidou still needed to keep in with the traditional Gaullists. But on January 19, 1972, he found himself presented with a situation in which it was very difficult for him to keep Chaban-Delmas on as prime minister.

It was then that the satirical paper *Le Canard Enchaîné*, which since its establishment in 1876 has always enjoyed extraordinarily privileged access to matters normally regarded as highly secret and strictly personal, published documents proving that Chaban-Delmas had not paid any income tax for several years. There was nothing illegal about this. He had merely taken advantage of an arrangement known as *l'avoir fiscal*, roughly speaking of tax credits, which was available to anyone with a skilled accountant. But it didn't look too good, especially in the light of the forthcoming parliamentary elections, due to be held on March 2 and 10, 1973. In spite of Chaban-Delmas's insistence that he would win the elections anyway, Pompidou exercised his presidential prerogative and replaced him with another equally traditional if less athletic Gaullist, Pierre Messmer, a former colonial governor who had also been in the resistance movement.

Pompidou kept Messmer as his prime minister until his own premature death cut short one of the most brilliant careers in French politics at the early age of 63. His illness, a rare version of leukaemia known as myelomatosis or Kahler's syndrome, had begun to affect him as early as 1968, when it had been treated with cortisone. In August 1972, after his doctors had diagnosed what was wrong with him, his physical appearance began to suggest that he was ill, and from that time onwards he began, as he wrote to one of his friends, to suffer the torments of the damned for twenty-four hours out of twenty-four. But no official announcement was made of his illness until his death on April 2, 1974, and comments then varied between praise for his courage in carrying on as he did, and criticism for having stayed in office when he was so seriously ill as to be unable to do anything useful.

Alain Poher, as president of the Senate, thus had to step in again as a temporary measure. Had he been able to count on the two-thirds majority in the Assemblée Nationale and the Senate necessary to bring about such a reform, Pompidou would have reduced the presidential mandate from seven to five years. He is the only president to have made a serious attempt to alter this aspect of the Constitution, and would almost certainly have done so had he lived to complete his own seven-year mandate, which was not due to expire until April 1976. As it is, he left behind him an uncompleted mission, but one which more

than stands comparison with the achievements either of his predecessor or of the three men who have followed him.

Perhaps most importantly, he ensured that the institutions of the
Fifth Republic survived the departure of its creator. One of the major
criticisms which François Mitterrand and others on the left had made
of the Constitution of the Fifth Republic was that it was intended to
give power to only one man, Charles de Gaulle. There was, in
Mitterrand's view, no more chance of the Fifth Republic being
governed by anyone else than there had been of the empire of
Napoleon I living on after he had gone. The ease with which
Pompidou took over was both a tribute to the skill as constitutional
lawyers of those who, under de Gaulle's direction, had drafted the
Constitution, and a reflection of his own intelligence and popularity.
The Fifth Republic was no longer the product of what had, in the last
analysis, been the military *coup d'état* of May 13, 1958 which had
enabled de Gaulle to come back to power. It was now, as befitted the
France of the twentieth century, a democratic régime run by civilians.
A schoolmaster turned banker was now in charge. There would, henceforth, be no more politicians appearing on television in uniform.

It was not only in May 1968 that Pompidou had prevented the auto-
cratic side of de Gaulle's nature from leading him into serious error. In
April 1962, General Jouhaud, who had played a leading role in the
attempted putsch of April 1961, and had been one of the leaders of
the Organisation de l'Armée Secrète, had been sentenced to death. De
Gaulle, furious that the head of the OAS, Raoul Salan, had been
merely sentenced to life imprisonment by the military court which had
judged him, was determined that Jouhaud should not get away with it.
Only Pompidou's determination and powers of persuasion, reinforced
in the last resort by the threat to resign, saved de Gaulle from an act
which would have put off for many years the reconciliation between
the Fifth Republic and the French army which was essential if the
régime was to put the past behind it. In 1961, as in 1960, de Gaulle
had defeated the army. It was, in many way, his greatest triumph. But
magnanimity in politics, as Burke observed in 1775 in his Speech on
Conciliation with America, 'is not seldom the greatest wisdom. And a
great empire and little minds go ill together'. In April 1962 as in May
1968, it was Pompidou, not de Gaulle who showed the wisdom.

In June 1969, on forming his first government with Jacques
Chaban-Delmas as prime minister, Pompidou chose to have as foreign
minister one of the best-known of the 'gaullistes historiques', Maurice
Schumann. Until the first 'cohabitation' of 1986, there had always
been something fictional in the statement in Article 8 of the 1958

Constitution that the president 'appoints the other members of the Government on the proposal of the Prime Minister'. Nobody contested the right of the president to choose who would and who would not be in the government, and there was a touch of de Gaulle's own tactics in Pompidou's decision to have Schumann at the Quai d'Orsay. When de Gaulle had wanted to show how impossible the policy of L'Algérie Française had become, he had placed Michel Debré at the head of the government which was to give Algeria its independence. When Pompidou wished to reverse de Gaulle's policy on British entry into the European Economic Community, he chose to have his policy carried out by the man who had, between 1940 and 1944, been the voice of Gaullist France on the BBC.

There is no evidence that Schumann was unhappy about this. Unlike de Gaulle, he liked the English. He had also been a founder member of the Mouvement Républicain Populaire, one of whose main articles of belief had been the need for European unification. On May 15, 1962, it was the ministers from the MRP who had resigned in protest against de Gaulle's attack in his press conference on the idea of a federal Europe. Schumann got on well with the main British negotiator, Edward Heath, and on 1971 became the first French foreign minister for eight years to pay an official visit to London. It was as a result of his efforts, and of Pompidou's own initiative, that on June 22, 1971 the treaty was signed, setting out the conditions on which Great Britain, Denmark and the Republic of Ireland were to become members of the EEC on January 1, 1973.

On April 23, 1972, a referendum was held in France on the conditions for European expansion and the entry of the United Kingdom. Unlike de Gaulle, and perhaps fortunately, Pompidou did not link his own position as president of the Republic to its outcome. Admittedly there was a majority of 67.7 per cent of those voting in favour of the proposed enlargement. But there was also a record number of abstentions: 39.9 per cent of the electorate did not bother to vote, and there was also a record number of spoilt or blank papers – 7.1 per cent. Many years later, on September 20, 1992, only 51 per cent of those voting in a referendum on the Maastricht treaty said 'yes', and it may well be that there is less support among grassroots opinion in France for an increasingly united Europe than is sometimes suggested.

Pompidou himself was a convinced European. His main ambition was to make France a more efficient industrialised nation, and he saw in the increased competition brought about by the common market one of the best ways of bringing this about. He was also shrewd enough to see that the economic weakness of the United Kingdom was unlikely to offer a serious threat to the Franco–German condominium which de Gaulle's two vetoes had sought to perpetuate, and that Britain was more likely to become an open market for French exports than a serious rival in the European market. Politically, he took the widely held if perhaps not entirely accurate view that while Europe would be difficult with Great Britain, it was impossible without her.

Pompidou's enthusiasm for rapid industrialisation did not always increase his popularity. His success in persuading Électricité de France to build American-style nuclear generators did not endear him to traditional Gaullists. The creation in December 1973 of the enormous steel-making centre at Fos was almost entirely his initiative, but was no more acceptable to the ecologist lobby than his love affair with the motor car. This led not only to an increase in the number of autoroutes, but also to the danger that Paris would soon cease to be a city for pedestrians and be wholly dominated by traffic. But this was the price which he thought that France had to pay for its continued industrialisation, and it is significant that the president who had the lowest starting point in French society should have been the one most determined to enable the French to get richer.

Pompidou would have been the last person to claim exclusive credit for the fact that between his election in June 1969 and his death in April 1974, France enjoyed a growth rate of 6 per cent per year, higher than that of any other European country. The accompanying increase of 25 per cent in the standard of living of its inhabitants owed as much to the foundations laid by the excellent planning undertaken under the Fourth Republic as it did to any initiative taken either by Pompidou or by de Gaulle. But Pompidou made a more conscious and more determined effort to continue it than de Gaulle had ever done. In this respect, as in others, he was the ideal man to carry on after the charismatic founder of the Fifth Republic.

3 Valéry Giscard d'Estaing
The ambitious nephew

Generalities

In a republic, where there is no monarch to serve as fount of honour, there is only one way for a socially ambitious middle-class family to acquire a tincture of nobility: by reviving the name of an aristocratic house thought to be extinct. This is what René and Edmond Giscard, the father and uncle of the third president of the Fifth Republic, sought to do in 1923, applying initially to add the name 'de La Tour Fondue' to that of Giscard.

They were, however, prevented by a surviving member of the 'de La Tour Fondue' family, who exercised her right to the exclusive possession of the name. They consequently made a different claim, that of being the descendants of Count Charles Henri d'Estaing (1729–94), the admiral who had commanded the French navy during the war of American independence. It was a claim based upon the fact that the admiral's illegitimate niece, Lucie-Madeleine d'Estaing, had had a daughter, Gilberte-Elizabeth-Marguerite who had, in 1818, married their great-grandfather, Marie-Barthélemy Martial Giscard. The claim could be formulated only because the admiral himself, who had also commanded the National Guard at Versailles in 1789, had been guillotined by the revolutionaries in 1784, and had no direct living descendants.

The title is not recognised as valid by the Association de la noblesse française, and it was only because he was president of the Republic that Valéry Giscard d'Estaing was given honorary membership, during his visit to the United States in 1976, of the Association de Cincinnati, an organisation which groups together the descendants of the French families who fought on the American side in the American war of independence. His personal claim to membership had earlier been turned down twice.[1]

Giscard d'Estaing married into a family very similar to his own. The paternal great-grandfather of Anne-Aymone Sauvage des Brantes, whom he married on December 23, 1952, had originally been plain M. Sauvage, just as Giscard d'Estaing's father had started life as plain M. Giscard. Monsieur Sauvage, however, had also acquired the right to a more noble appellation. By a decree dating back to August 6, 1860, in the middle of the Second Empire, he became M. Sauvage des Brantes, so that when, in 1952, at the age of 19, she married the 24-year-old Valéry Giscard d'Estaing, it was with an aristocratic patronymic which sounded just as impressive as that of her husband. She was also of a more authentic ancient lineage through her mother, la Princesse Aymone de Faucigny-Lucinge, as well as being, through her aunt, Charlotte de Faucigny-Lucinge, related to the right-wing historian and essayist Alfred Fabre-Luce, in whose salon she first met the future president of the Republic.

In accordance with what were then the customs of her class, she did not receive the same kind of education as her husband. She was not allowed to take her baccalauréat, and studied fine arts at the École du Louvre. Like those of their parents, the names of their four children – Valérie-Anne, born in November 1953; Henri, born in October 1956; Louise-Joachim, born in 1958; and Jacinte, born in 1960 – have an impeccably aristocratic ring to them.

At lunches and dinners at the Élysée Palace, Giscard d'Estaing had himself served first. This is said always to have been the monarchical tradition in France, and was observed by Félix Faure (1841–99; 1895–9), though only when receiving members of the Chambre des Députés who were, at the time, all men. De Gaulle also had himself served first when acting as head of state, though with the proviso that any other head of state present should be served at the same time. In private dinners at the Elysée, he had himself served last.[2] But when Giscard d'Estaing entertained Margaret Thatcher to lunch at the Élysée Palace in 1980, she was served after him. He was the president. She was merely a prime minister.

The social pretensions of the third president of the Fifth Republic make him intensely vulnerable to Frank Richards' remark to George Orwell in 1940 that 'foreigners *are* funny. They lack the sense of humour which is the special gift to our own chosen nation; and people without a sense of humour are always funny'.[3] In addition to being head of state, he prided himself on the possibility of being an illegitimate descendant, through a chambermaid later married off to a tax collector, of Louis XV (1710–74; 1715–74).

Giscard d'Estaing's politics were less eccentric than his social behaviour. For him, as for Georges Pompidou, the aim of politics was to provide a stable society in which people could get richer and live their lives with the minimum of interference from the state. There are few nobler political ambitions, and it is salutary to compare the fortunes of the France of the 1970s with those of Great Britain during the same period. While the gross national product of France increased by 21.1 per cent, that of Great Britain grew by only 2.1 per cent. It was also during the seven-year period during which Valéry Giscard d'Estaing was president of the Fifth Republic that the event took place which *L'Année Politique* for 1975 greeted as one of the most significant in European history: for the first time since the beginning of the industrial revolution, the per capita income of the inhabitants of France overtook that of the inhabitants of the United Kingdom.

Since these were the years in which the office of prime minister was held first of all by two grammar school boys, Edward Heath (1916–; 1970–4), Harold Wilson (1916–95; 1964–70; 1974–6), and then by a former tax-officer, James Callaghan (1912–; 1976–81), who had left school at the age of 16, there might indeed seem to be a case for electing to the supreme office of state first of all a schoolmaster turned banker, followed by a technocrat whose educational achievements are more impressive than his aristocratic ancestry.

1926–74

It was not as a member of a ruling class basing its claims to exercise power through birth that Valéry Giscard d'Estaing entered politics. He did so because he was member of the technocratic élite trained at the École Nationale d'Administration, an institution whose importance can also be judged from the fact that six of the fifteen men and the one woman to have held the office of prime minister in the Fifth Republic are former students.[4]

By the age of 23, Giscard d'Estaing had acquired the distinction, still unusual even in this super élite in French society, of having received a scientific education as well as the intense training in law, administration and management dispensed to the graduates of the École Nationale d'Administration. They have generally studied law or social science before spending their two and a half years at l'ÉNA, but Giscard d'Estaing, having done well during the academic year 1943–4 in the special classes in science and mathematics at the lycée Louis-le-Grand, had won a place at the École Polytechnique.

He took this up in 1945, having taken part, as a volunteer, in the last stages of the European war, and won both the croix de guerre and the Bronze Star Medal. He consequently felt quite at home in an institution originally founded in 1794 for the training of artillery officers. It now trains engineers and scientists for all walks of life in French society, and it was certainly a great advantage to Giscard d'Estaing not only to have received a scientific education at the École Polytechnique before going to the École Nationale d'Administration, but also for this fact to be very widely known. For the more self-consciously republican electors who voted for him in 1974, it helped to outweigh the insistence which his family had chosen to lay on their recently acquired aristocratic origins.

For Giscard d'Estaing was undoubtedly a man whose achievements fitted the criterion laid down in the last two sentences of Article VI of the 1789 Déclaration des droits de l'homme et du citoyen when it said that the only distinctions which should enable members of a society to take part in the creation of its laws are their own 'virtues and talents'. He had proved his manhood on the field of battle, and his mental capacity in one of the most competitive educational systems known to man. And, perhaps even more importantly, he had served the state for some twenty years as a democratically elected politician concerning himself with what is perhaps the most important issue in a modern state, that of public finance and economic policy.

In 1945, Giscard d'Estaing had done well enough in the *concours de sortie de l'École Polytechnique* to exercise the right to proceed directly to the École Nationale d'Administration, and was the first *polytechnicien* to do so. At l'ÉNA itself, he was to achieve the exceptionally high mark of 19/20 for the period of work experience (*stage*), which he had spent at the Banque de France, and came out sixth in the final *concours de sortie*. Since the written papers are marked anonymously, and the name of the candidate is never pronounced at the oral, there can have been no question of favouritism. Even if the examiners had recognised him, they would have been sufficiently imbued with *l'esprit républicain* (the Republican ethic) to be more ready to penalise than to reward the holder of an aristocratic name.

The fact of having been placed in what is known as *la botte*, that is to say the first fifteen candidates in the *concours de sortie*, gave Giscard d'Estaing the right to enter one of the Grands Corps de l'État. He chose l'Inspection des Finances, but did not stay there long. On June 17, 1954, he took what is known in its full administrative form as *une mise en disponibilité pour convenance personnelle*, and was appointed as special adviser to the *cabinet* of Edgar Faure, finance minister in the government of Pierre Mendès France. On January 2, 1956, he was elected to the seat in the Puy-de-Dôme which his grandfather on his mother's side of the family, Jacques Bardoux (1874–1959), now aged 82, had agreed to hand over to him.

As a député, he was able to benefit from his *mise en disponibilité* for as long as he liked. He nevertheless found it useful to go back briefly to his *corps d'origine* on January 9, 1966. Although he stayed only fifteen months, leaving again on April 3, 1967, it enabled him to keep in touch with the world of the higher civil service in a way which might perhaps have been found, in English-speaking democracies, slightly suspect in a man so obviously committed to a full-time political career. He did not make this temporary return to the civil service because he needed his salary. He has a large private fortune, and owns two castles, in addition to an *hôtel particulier* (large private house) in Paris, with fifteen rooms.

One of these castles came to him on his marriage to Anne-Aymone Sauvage de Brantes, who added to her aristocratic origins the more solid advantage of being one of the great-granddaughters of the Schneider family, who in the nineteenth century owned most of the steel mills in the east of France. It is also a reflection of the equality of treatment which the Republic metes out to all its citizens that Madame Giscard d'Estaing is also officially registered as a farmer (*exploitante agricole*) in the Département du Loir-et-Cher. She thus has the right not only to government subsidies for the running of her property but also to a farmer's pension when she reaches retirement age.

On his election to the Assemblée Nationale in 1956, Giscard d'Estaing joined the formation which, in the coded language of French politics, indicated its ambition to combine right-wing sympathies with a social conscience by calling itself Le Groupe des Indépendants et Paysans d'Action Sociale. He then moved slightly to the left by linking himself with a number of younger députés associated with Pierre Mendès France, before adding his name to those lending their support, in November 1956, to the attempt by the president of the Republic, René Coty, to bring de Gaulle back to power. On June 1, 1958, he was one of the 329 députés who voted in favour of giving full powers to de Gaulle to govern France and to prepare the Constitution of the Fifth Republic. On November 30 of the same year he was re-elected député for the constituency of Clermont-Nord et Sud-Ouest.

One of the features of the Fifth Republic which reflects de Gaulle's attempt to reduce the influence of political parties is the requirement that a député appointed to a ministerial post should cease to sit and vote in the Chamber. When, therefore on January 9, 1959, at the age of thirty-two, he was appointed Secrétaire d'État au budget (minister of state for financial matters) in the government formed by Michel Debré on de Gaulle's official assumption of the office of President of the Republic, Giscard d'Estaing was obliged to hand over his seat to his *suppléant*. Since, however, he still theoretically remained a député, he continued to remain on leave from the civil service.

On January 19, 1962, when Michel Debré was replaced by Georges Pompidou, he was promoted to a full ministerial post, as 'ministre des finances et du budget'. He was, however, as he put it, dismissed 'like a servant', after de Gaulle had succeeded in being elected president by universal suffrage on December 12, 1965. In de Gaulle's view, it was the tight money policy (*plan de stabilisation*) which Giscard d'Estaing had introduced in September 1962 which was partly responsible for the fact that he was not, as he had expected to be, elected president on the first ballot of December 5, 1965. While the restrictions on credit involved in this plan had brought inflation down, they had also put a brake on industrial production, as well as alienating some of de Gaulle's natural supporters by imposing a value added tax on the sale of land and property owned for less than five years. When Georges Pompidou had suggested the adoption of a more Keynesian policy of higher public expenditure in order to win over industrialists and trade union leaders before the presidential election, Giscard d'Estaing had dismissed the idea as 'electioneering', and won the argument.

It was after his dismissal as finance minister in January 1966 that Giscard d'Estaing began to adopt a more critical attitude towards de Gaulle. He had already, in December 1962, been part of a parliamentary group known as Les Républicains Indépendants, and in May 1966 he established it as a political party, La Fédération Nationale des Républicains Indépendants. The fact that he did this during the brief period when he was exercising his right to go back to being a serving member of the Inspection des Finances is again a reflection of the ease with which members of the higher civil service in France can quite openly engage in political activity while still in office. The same is true of his re-election as one of the députés for the Puy-de-Dôme on March 5, 1967, a month before he left his *corps* again, this time permanently.

At this point in his career, Giscard d'Estaing even distanced himself from Pompidou, to the point of letting it be known that he might consider standing as a presidential candidate when the time came. After de Gaulle's 'Vive le Québec libre', on July 24, 1967, he openly attacked what he called 'l'exercice solitaire du pouvoir' (the solitary exercise of power). During the events of May 1968, he suggested that Pompidou, whom he held responsible for the failure to implement the reforms which might have avoided the student uprising, should resign, though without going so far as to suggest that he might replace him.

Another distinctive feature of French political life, and one which is frequently contested by the French themselves, is the practice known as *le cumul des mandats*, the arrangement whereby a politician used to be able to be at one and the same time a député, a senator, or even a minister, and combine this with election to municipal office, and/or to membership of departmental and regional councils. Between 1956 and 1974, Giscard d'Estaing was conseiller général (town councillor) for the canton de Rochefort-Montagne, in the Puy-de-Dôme, and it was from the steps of the town hall of the town of Chamalières that he advised local electors, and through them the French nation in general, to vote 'no' in the April 1969 referendum of the reform of the Senate. It was also at Chamalières that during his first three years as president of the Republic, between 1974 and 1977, he kept in touch with what he saw as his local roots by being elected conseiller municipal.

After his fellow members of the Républicains Indépendants had advised him not to stand against Pompidou in the 1969 presidential election, Giscard d'Estaing gave Pompidou his full support. He did this, it is said, in return for the promise of a renewed appointment as minister of finance if Pompidou were elected. The promise was kept, and Giscard d'Estaing held the post from June 22, 1969 to May 21 1974, when he resigned on his election as president.

It was a period of continued prosperity in France. The inflationary tendencies which were to dominate the 1970s were still being held in check by the fairly cautious policies favoured by Giscard d'Estaing, often against Pompidou's own preference for a more expansionist approach. Unlike the United Kingdom, France maintained a slight excess in its external balance of payments. Wages kept slightly ahead of inflation, with the *Salaire Minimum Interprofessionnel de Croissance* (SMIC) increasing in 1972 by 12 per cent as opposed to a price increase of 7 per cent, and an economic growth rate staying at an average of 5.3 per cent a year. In 1973, before the effects of the sudden increase in oil prices decreed by the Organization of Petroleum-Exporting Countries (OPEC) in September of that year had begun to make its effects felt, industrial production rose by a further 9 per cent.

But the beginnings of the economic crisis which was to put an end to the prosperity of what the French economist Jean Fourastié later called 'les trente glorieuses', the years of continued economic growth which followed the end of the second world war in 1945, were already at hand. For historians of a progressive disposition, the beginnings of the inflation which was to be one of the major factors in putting an end of this prosperity is summarised by Tom Wolfe in *The Bonfire of the Vanities* (1987), when he writes of how the United States 'began printing money to finance the war in Vietnam', and adds 'before anyone, before even Johnson, knew what was happening, a worldwide inflation had begun'.

After having laid the blame clearly on the United States, Wolfe then refers to the explanation offered by historians of a more conservative disposition, stating that 'when the Arabs suddenly jacked up oil prices in the early 1970s, in no time, markets of all sorts became heaving crapshots'. This price increase was as part of their campaign against Israel, and this passage from *The Bonfire of the Vanities* then moves on to an analysis of the effects of the financial move with which Giscard d'Estaing's name is most closely associated, the loan which he launched in 1972. This, as Tom Wolfe points out, 'had an interesting feature: it was backed by gold. So as the price of gold went up and down, so did the price of the Giscard', and it will be recalled from the text of *The Bonfire of the Vanities* that its anti-hero, Sherman McCoy, is hoping to make a major killing by buying and selling it at the right time.[5]

Had his career not ended with the tragic abruptness that it did, Sherman would undoubtedly have made his killing. Although the Giscard was not directly indexed on the price of gold, it was based on the relationship between gold and the European Unit of Account. When the Jamaica agreement of 1976 gave permanent form to the system of floating exchange rates first introduced when President Nixon cut the link between the dollar and gold in August 1971, the price of gold, and consequently of the Giscard, rose dramatically.

When, therefore, the French government had to repay the investors who had bought the bond, the final cost to tax-payers was quite a high one. Although the Giscard had brought in, when issued, 6. 5 milliards (six and a half thousand million francs) to the French treasury, it finally cost, when it became repayable in 1988, 100 milliards. On first being told that Giscard d'Estaing was going to launch a loan under his own name, de Gaulle is alleged to have said 'en effet, un joli nom d'emprunt'. It was one of his better puns.

It is nevertheless hard to hold Giscard d'Estaing personally responsible for the fiasco of his loan, or to argue from the better performance for the French treasury of the *emprunt Pinay*, the loan launched in 1952 by Antoine Pinay (1891–1991) when he was Président du Conseil under the Fourth Republic, that it is better to have the nation's finances run by the provincial owner of a successful tanning factory than by one of the most highly qualified graduates of the École

Nationale d'Administration. Pinay had the good fortune to launch his loan at a time when inflation was relatively low, and the price of gold therefore fairly stable.

As finance minister, Giscard d'Estaing took a number of steps to improve the daily life of ordinary French people. He may, as his critics allege, have done so in a spirit of aristocratic condescension, and in order to strengthen his chances of becoming Pompidou's successor. He made it easier for ordinary citizens to buy shares on the stock exchange, and took steps to realise de Gaulle's ideal of 'la participation' by initiating the setting up of schemes to enable workers to share in the profits of their firms.

In 1966, he also took an important step towards making it easier for ordinary employees to deal with the problem of paying their income tax by the introduction of the French equivalent of the British Pay As You Earn (PAYE) system, *la mensualisation de l'impôt*. Instead of having to find a lump sum three times a year, the tax-payer can choose to have his or her income tax deducted directly at source. It is, however, a reflection of the relative slowness with which administrative changes are welcomed in France that by 1986, only 35 per cent of French tax-payers had chosen this particular option.[6]

1974–81

Giscard d'Estaing had two main rivals in the first round of voting on May 5, 1974 to elect the third president of the Fifth Republic. They were the Gaullist Jacques Chaban-Delmas (1915–), who had served as prime minister under Georges Pompidou between 1969 and 1971; and the socialist François Mitterrand (1916–96), who was making his second attempt to be elected, this time as the representative of a left united enough to receive the support of the Communist Party. There were also another nine candidates recognised as eligible to stand. Each of them had paid a deposit of 10,000 francs (roughly £1,000 or $1,600) and secured the signature of at least 500 French citizens occupying an elected office, whether as député, sénateur, conseiller régional, conseiller municipal, or maire.

Since there is nothing to stop an elected representative from signing the application form of more than one candidate, and since there are 36,000 *communes* in France, each with its own mayor, such signatures are not all that difficult to obtain. The marginal candidates included two representatives from the non-Communist extreme left, Arlette Laguiller (1940–), from the Trotskyite Lutte ouvrière, standing for the second time, who received 591,339 votes, and Alain Krivine (1941–), from the even more radical Ligue communiste révolutionnaire. He had been excluded from the Parti Communiste Français in 1966, and was at the time doing his military service.

It was only after a special ruling by the Conseil d'État that Alain Krivine could be recognised as eligible, and he received 92,719 votes. The man who received the largest number after the three main candidates, Jean Royer (1920–) made his appeal to the small businessmen and shopkeepers who had earlier lent their support to more extremist opponents of high taxation and government interference such as Pierre Poujade (January 12, 1920–) and Gérard Nicoud (1931–), and received 808,825 votes. Unemployment was still well under the half million mark, and racism consequently a more inhibited feature of French working-class and lower-middle-class society. Jean-Marie Le Pen (1928–) received only 189,304 votes, a score which was to increase considerably in later years.

The surprise felt by Europeans at the relatively low turn out for American presidential elections becomes more explicable when the large number of people voting in French presidential elections is taken into account. Eighty-five per cent of the electorate turned out for the first round of voting, and there were two major surprises: the relatively low score of the Gaullist candidate Chaban-Delmas in relation to Giscard d'Estaing, 14.55 per cent of the electorate as against 32.93 per cent; and the fact that the candidate who polled the most votes was François Mitterrand, with 43.35 per cent. Gaullism, now that de Gaulle and Pompidou were both dead, and the Constitution of the Fifth Republic seen as a permanent feature of the French political landscape, seemed to be losing out to a more relaxed form of conservatism. Socialism also looked a more attractive prospect than it had since the 1950s, and the most respectable and reliable French newspaper, *Le Monde*, gave its support to Mitterrand.

The second ballot, on May 19, 1974, confirmed his impression. Chaban-Delmas told his supporters to vote for Giscard d'Estaing, as did Jean Royer and, more embarrassingly, Jean-Marie Le Pen. The left, including the communist-dominated trade union grouping, La Confédération Générale du Travail (CGT), came out in favour of Mitterrand, and the result might have been even closer if the major teachers union, La Fédération de l'Éducation Nationale, and the socialist trade unions grouped under Force Ouvrière, had supported him more enthusiastically. As it was, Giscard d'Estaing won by a margin of only 344,399 votes out of the 25,819,613 total cast, or 50.66 per cent as against 49.33 per cent out of the 86.17 per cent of the French population voting.

Once elected, he took up his new functions on May 27, and did so in a rather self-consciously informal and undramatic style. After driving himself to the Ministère de l'Économie et des Finances in his own car, he walked from the Place Clemenceau to the Palais de l'Élysée along the Avenue Marigny. There, he was met by the president of the Senate, Alain Poher, who had once again fulfilled the duty laid down for him in the Constitution and been acting as president since Pompidou's death on April 2. This time, however, he had not been a candidate himself for the office of president. He was accompanied by Pierre Messmer, whom Pompidou had appointed prime minister on March 2.

Unlike de Gaulle and Pompidou, who had worn a morning coat for the official ceremony of induction, Giscard d'Estaing wore a lounge suit. He did not exercise the traditional right of having the official *collier du grand maître de la Légion d'honneur* placed round his neck, but simply wore the insignia in his button hole. Whereas the official photograph of de Gaulle and Pompidou had shown them in a highly formal pose, wearing a morning coat, and with the *collier* and cross of the Legion of Honour fully visible, Giscard d'Estaing chose to have himself photographed with simply his head and shoulders showing, in an ordinary suit, against the background of the white section of the tricolore.

This desire to show the president rather as American presidents are shown in their official photographs was part of Giscard d'Estaing's ideal self-image. Like them, he wanted to be seen as a concerned senior executive whose genuine power enabled him to dispense, at least in public, with semi-monarchical flummery. His model was John F. Kennedy (1917–63), whom he resembled primarily by his youth. Kennedy, at the age of 43, was the youngest man to be elected president of the United States. At 44, Giscard d'Estaing was the second youngest to be elected president of France, the youngest being Casimir-Périer, who was elected in 1894 at the age of 43. *Newsweek* for 1975 did indeed call Giscard d'Estaing 'le Kennedy gaulois', a more flattering appellation than the one bestowed on him by the satirical paper *Le Canard enchaîné*, which called him 'Sa Suffisance Giscard d'Estaing' (His Self-Satisfaction Giscard d'Estaing).

Rather strangely, considering his aristocratic background and the monarchical behaviour which he was to adopt in the Elysée Palace itself, Giscard d'Estaing let it be known that one of his favourite hobbies was playing the accordion, an unobjectionable but very working-class pastime. He reduced the rhythm at which the *Marseillaise* was played from that of a triumphant military march to that of a gentle saunter, and announced that he would be happy to accept invitations to dine with ordinary French families. On the morning of December 24, 1975, he invited a number of slightly astonished Parisian dustmen to take breakfast with him at the Élysée Palace.

Central to the demands of the 1968 student rebellion was a more easy-going and liberal society. Unlike François Mitterrand, whose role in 1968 will be discussed in the following chapter, Giscard d'Estaing did not endorse the ambition to overthrow the Gaullist state which inspired the revolutionaries of 1968. However, his actions as president did help to bring about some of their more rational objectives, and to do so in a way which cast doubt on de Gaulle's much quoted dictum that 'La France ne fait de réformes que dans la foulée d'une révolution (France carries out reforms only in the aftermath of a revolution). Giscard d'Estaing did so in the calm atmosphere created by an electoral victory carried out in the normal conditions of the liberal society which it was his declared intention to maintain and improve.

One of the ways in which the French state had taken upon itself, since 1920 onwards, to interfere with the private lives of its citizens was in the penalties imposed on anyone who sold or advertised contraceptives. This law had not had much effect on the phenomenon known as *la dénatalité française*, the failure of the French population to grow at the same rate as that of its European neighbours. Between 1880 and 1910, the population of Germany had grown by 43 per cent as against a mere 5 per cent in France, and the law of 1920 had been aimed at avoiding the situation which arose in 1914, when 40 million French people faced 80 million Germans. It did not work, and even after some of the shortfall had been made up by immigration, there was still a net decline in the French population between 1919 and 1939.

There had, however, been a considerable improvement since 1945, almost certainly brought about by the greater prosperity of 'les trente glorieuses', as well, perhaps, as by a generous policy of family allowances. By the 1960s, the French population had risen to over 50 million, a fact which encouraged a feeling of demographic self-confidence as well as the realisation that France had a good deal of catching up to do in an area where other countries were treating their citizens as responsible adults. After all, if the United States, the United Kingdom, Germany and the Scandinavian countries had stopped interfering in this aspect of the private life of their citizens, it was high time that the French Republic, which put the word liberty first in its official slogan, should do the same.

The French equivalent of Margaret Thatcher's phrase about 'rolling back the frontiers of the state' did not begin to be popular until the late 1980s. It was then that conservative politicians began to talk about 'le moins d'état', and to do so in order to argue that the government should stop interfering in the workings of the free market. For the average French citizen, however, especially if she happened to be a woman, a more immediate and essential application of 'le moins d'état' can be said have taken place with a measure which had already been formally approved by parliament in 1967, but which Giscard d'Estaing did a great deal to help put into practical and widespread effect.

It was on December 20, 1967 that Lucien Neuwirth, a young Gaullist député belonging to what was then known as the Union pour la Nouvelle République (UNR) finally succeeded in having a private member's bill (*proposition de loi*) abrogating the law of 1920, approved by the Chambre des Députés. But because it was a private member's bill, it did not have the support from the government which it needed to come into force, and for its dispositions to be widely known. It was only in early 1971 that the final *décrets d'application* were published, and not until December 2, 1972 that the *Journal Officiel* published two texts authorising the opening of advisory centres for birth control. And it was not until 1975, in the first year of Giscard d'Estaing's presidency, that the crucial steps were taken to make artificial contraception fully legal, to have the cost of the technique chosen repayable by the social security system, and to make advice available by the provision of openly advertised family planning centres.[7]

The pressure which Giscard d'Estaing exerted in this context was as crucial as the effort made by Jacques Chirac, after his election in May 1995, to have Maurice Papon finally brought to trial for his actions as secrétaire général de la Gironde under the Vichy government in the 1940s, and illustrates an important aspect of presidential power in France. The president may not always be able to bring about the changes he would like, but he can be very influential in preventing things happening of which he disapproves. Although de Gaulle agreed not to oppose Neuwirth's bill, he was not particularly keen on the idea, any more than was Pompidou. It is this which accounts for the slowness with which it was implemented, just as the anxiety of François Mitterrand not to revive painful memories of the Vichy government explains the delay in putting Maurice Papon on trial.

Greater freedom in sexual matters had been, understandably in the light of the youth of most of the participants, one of the basic demands of the student rebels of 1968, together with other changes such as greater equality between the sexes and less state control over radio and television. On January 17, 1975, a further step was taken towards what is seen as an enlightened attitude on sexual matters with the legalisation of *l'interruption volontaire de grossesse* (IVG – voluntary termination of pregnancy), a measure introduced in Great Britain in 1967 and in the United States by the Roe versus Wade case of 1972.

Although it was not until 1982 that women choosing to terminate an unwanted pregnancy in France could have the costs of the operation met by the social security system, the 1975 decision was seen as an important step whereby a change in private behaviour was reflected in the legal system in France. For there were, according to the supporters of the measure introduced by Simone Veil (1927–) while minister of health, as many illegal abortions in France as there were live births. Since, they argued, such operations were going to take place anyway, they should do so with the minimum of risk to the mother. It was, as they also pointed out, a question of social justice. Most of the women placing themselves at risk by having a backstreet abortion did so because they were too poor to go and have the operation carried out by qualified medical practitioners in England.

Simone Veil was minister of health between 1974 and 1979, and her presence in both the government of Jacques Chirac, who resigned as prime minister in August 1986, and in the first two governments of his successor, Raymond Barre, reflects the nature of some of the other changes encouraged in French society by Giscard d'Estaing. Neither de Gaulle nor Pompidou had appointed a woman to any governmental post higher than that of secrétaire d'état, the equivalent of the relatively junior British minister of state, and neither had given an important government post to a Jew. Simone Veil's Jewishness had been unambiguously recognised both by the Vichy government and by the Nazis when she was deported to Auschwitz on April 13, 1944, and transferred to Bergen-Belsen, where she was liberated on April 15, 1945. When she was appointed as ministre de la santé in May 1974, she was the first woman to attain full ministerial rank in France.

The vote of what is officially known as 'la loi Veil' had been preceded by an intense campaign in which 123 famous women, including Simone de Beauvoir, Delphine Seyrig, Jeanne Moreau and Catherine Deneuve, published an open letter on April 6, 1971 declaring that they had had a pregnancy terminated and challenging the government to take them to court. As in the case of the detailed implementation of the 'loi Neuwirth', it is very doubtful if an executive headed even by as enlightened a Gaullist as Jacques Chaban-Delmas would have legalised abortion.

Although it is difficult to see de Gaulle himself as a traditional conservative, the Gaullist party has never been noted for its ambition to liberalise French society. There were also a number of other measures introduced during the Giscard presidency which helped to improve the position of women in what had, traditionally, been a very male-dominated society. It was during the Giscard presidency, in 1975, that divorce became possible by mutual consent, and that the article in the Code Napoléon of 1804 stating that 'le domicile de la femme est celui de son mari' (the wife's residence is that of her husband) was changed so that both partners in the marriage had an equal right to decide where they lived.

In 1977, both men and women received the right to take leave in order to look after their children. In 1980, it became illegal to sack a woman because she was pregnant, and women obtained the right to take sixteen weeks' paid leave in order to have a baby as well as the right to go back to their former job if they wished to do so. Other measures aimed at improving the standard of living and legal rights of ordinary citizens included the reduction from 65 to 60 of the age at which anyone having worked thirty-seven and a half years could draw their pension, while at the other end of the age scale, the age at which French citizens could vote in elections was reduced in July 1974 to 18.

Giscard d'Estaing did not share all of Georges Pompidou's enthusiasm for industrial progress, and was especially critical of his transport policy. This had involved, in addition to the encouragement of more motorways, the construction of *la voie expresse de la rive gauche*, and the consequent total exclusion of pedestrians from the left bank of the Seine. The cancellation of this project by Giscard d'Estaing, like his support for the *Projet Galley* establishing stricter limits on the density of building in Paris, was one of the first victories for the ecology lobby, as well as another illustration of how effective an intervention by the president in power could be. On August 9, 1978, an event took place which offered a reminder of how minutely the French state had traditionally concerned itself with the details of the economic life of the nation. For the first time in over a century, the price of bread ceased to be fixed by the central government.

General de Gaulle was remarkably sensitive about the dignity both of his office and of his own personality. Whereas there had been, under the Third Republic, only four prosecutions against journalists for insulting the head of state, and only two in the Fourth Republic, there were over 500 between 1958 and 1969. And while there were far fewer under Georges Pompidou, Giscard d'Estaing inaugurated a practice followed under François Mitterrand by giving up the practice entirely. He also, as will be seen, did better than his successor in another important area of civil liberties. Telephone tapping by government agents was totally abolished under Giscard d'Estaing, only to be revived and widely practised under Mitterrand.

For de Gaulle, who in this respect if in no other, agreed with the politicians who ran the Third and Fourth Republics, the French were not sufficiently mature for what used to be referred to as 'l'information à l'anglo-saxonne' (Anglo-American style of broadcasting). It was, for de Gaulle, essential for the state to keep control of had become the most important of the media of mass communication. It was, after all, thanks to the radio that he had made himself known to the French between 1940 and 1944.

After a brief attempt at greater liberation, Georges Pompidou had gone back to an only slightly relaxed version of the earlier practice described in 1977 by Alain Peyrefitte in *Le Mal français*. For when Peyrefitte took over as minister of information in 1962, he found on his desk a series of buttons enabling him to summon the directors of the principal radio and television services and arrange with them what were to be the main items on the news broadcasts. Pompidou's first prime minister, Jacques Chaban-Delmas, tried to reform the system, but after he was replaced on July 17, 1972 by Pierre Messmer, the ministry of information, as J. R. Frears puts it, 'rose phoenix-like from the ashes'.[8]

The terror of French politicians as to what might happen if their opponents were allowed the kind of free access to radio and television regarded as the norm in Great Britain or the United States thus led to the practice, throughout the Fourth Republic and in the first fourteen years of the Fifth, whereby broadcasting continued to be dominated by the political party which happened to be in power. One of the more harmless and entertaining features of the events of May 1968 was the insistence of the journalists on the main French radio station, France-Inter, on playing the Beatles song *Yesterday*. The words seemed so appropriate that the song disappeared completely from all broadcasts when Gaullist order was restored, and it was in this area, as in that of the disappearance of the state's attempt to control people's sexual life, that the Giscard presidency showed how France could be made to take a few steps towards the more open and liberal society which Giscard d'Estaing described as his ideal in the book which he published in 1976, *La Démocratie française*.[9]

On July 8, 1974, the ORTF (Organisation de Radio et de Télévision Française), originally established in 1964, was divided into eight separate sections. This was a change from the previous system whereby the government had a 50 per cent membership of the *conseil d'administration* (board of governors) of the ORTF, appointed its chief administrators and examined all its accounts. But although the state could not exercise quite the same detailed control as in the past, it kept the final say as to how the money was spent. Giscard d'Estaing's admiration for English-speaking culture did not lead him to set up a board of governors with the same degree of independence as at the BBC, but it was a step in the right direction, and prepared the way for the more fundamental reforms carried out under the two Mitterrand presidencies.

Where Giscard d'Estaing's presidency was less successful, and where it is understandable that it should have been followed by the fourteen years of the socialist presidency of François Mitterrand, was in the economic performance of France, and there is a strong case for saying that this was not his fault. Between January 1, 1973 and January 1, 1974, the Organization of Petroleum-Exporting Countries (OPEC), brought the price of oil from $2.16 a barrel to $9 a barrel. A second increase, in 1979, after the revolution in Iran had driven out the Shah and replaced him by Ayotollah Khomeini, had the final effect of bringing the price of oil to $32 a barrel in 1981, with the result that it had, within eight years, been increased by a factor of almost 15.[10]

There was no secret about the reasons for this increase. Defeated on the field of battle in 1948 and 1967, and held to a draw in the fighting which began with the attack on Israel on the eve of Yom Kippur, on October 6, 1973, the Moslem states allied against Israel stuck to what was then the constant aim of their foreign policy: to destroy Israel and repeat the effects of Hitler's holocaust by driving all the Jews into the Mediterranean. Only the weapons employed changed, as they turned to economic warfare. After threatening to impose a total boycott on all states supporting or selling arms to Israel, they introduced selective price rises directed against pro-Israeli states, before making the price rises general.

Giscard d'Estaing thus came to power at a time when the economies of all Western countries were being placed under an immense strain imposed from outside. Only countries with an exceptionally robust economy, such Japan or the German Federal Republic, managed to keep their average annual inflation rate within single figures, and even that of Japan went up to 21.9 per cent in 1974 before falling back to an average of 6 per cent. That of France averaged 11 per cent a year between 1974 and 1980, a fairly honourable performance compared to that of the United Kingdom with 15 per cent, and roughly comparable to that of the United States.

Although Giscard d'Estaing could not bring himself to visit Israel, he followed Pompidou's approach of slightly softening the hostility to

Israel expressed by de Gaulle in 1967. In March 1980, in the course of a visit to the Gulf States, he said that Israel had the right to exist, but added that it would never have peaceful relations with its neighbours so long as it continued to occupy territories captured in the six-day war of 1967. However, neither this reservation nor his statement that the Palestine Liberation Organization should be a party to any negotiations on the Middle East enabled France to buy oil any cheaper. France still had to import 98 per cent of its oil, and thus to deal from a position of considerable weakness with the problems created for the world economy by the OPEC countries.

Giscard d'Estaing's critics rarely took account of these external factors when blaming him for the fact that unemployment rose so consistently, reaching 950,000 in 1976 and 1.5 million by the end of his presidency in 1981. For them, it was result of bad economic management, and it is true that the franc halved in value in relation to the mark between 1958 and 1967. But the political problems which Giscard d'Estaing had to face because of a world economic situation not of his making were heightened by the difficulty which he had in persuading Jacques Chirac, whom he had appointed prime minister on May 28, 1974, to accept the same vision of his role which Michel Debré, Georges Pompidou and Maurice Couve de Murville had under de Gaulle, and which Pierre Messmer had adopted from July 1972 onwards when he had replaced Jacques Chaban-Delmas.

De Gaulle's view of the relationship between the president and the prime minister was a simple one: the president took the major decisions, and the prime minister carried them out. There had already been indications that this might not always be a workable relationship when Chaban-Delmas succeeded in persuading the Assemblée Nationale to vote in favour of his ideas on 'la nouvelle société', only to find himself immediately asked to resign by Pompidou. But while it was fairly easy to understand why a traditionally-minded conservative such as Pompidou did not think much of what he saw as the rather vague ideas on 'la participation' which Chaban-Delmas had inherited from de Gaulle, it is more difficult to see precisely what divided Jacques Chirac and Giscard d'Estaing. Both were conservatives, the latter more centrist than the former, both were technocrats from l'ÉNA, and it was by no means clear what either of them would gain from breaking ranks.

It is true that Chirac was intensely ambitious, and that Giscard d'Estaing tended to treat him with something of the condescension which the ancestors he had chosen to adopt showed towards the steward who looked after their estates. But the only real difference which seems to have separated the two men was a question of parliamentary tactics. Chirac thought that Giscard d'Estaing ought to use the power which the Constitution gave him and dissolve the Assemblée Nationale, Giscard d'Estaing seemed quite happy with the one elected in 1973 and which he had inherited from Georges Pompidou. The parliamentary elections of March 4 and 11, 1973 had not given the neo-Gaullist Union pour la Nouvelle République the same absolute majority over all other parties which it had enjoyed as a result of the elections of June 23 and June 30, 1968. It was dependent on the votes of the 54 Républicains Indépendants, and although the president of the Fifth Republic was not, in theory, a party leader, this remained the party which Giscard d'Estaing had been instrumental in founding in 1966 and of which he had become president in May 1967. Jacques Chirac could therefore not count on enough députés who would be loyal to him to ensure victory in any conflict with the president. Giscard d'Estaing nevertheless thought that the UDR, which was coming increasingly under the control of Jacques Chirac, might achieve this if there were new elections, and it may have been for this reason that he refused to dissolve the National Assembly. The events of June 1997, when Chirac used the right to dissolve the Assemblée Nationale which he had inherited when elected president in 1995, showed that he is not always a very good judge of electoral form.

On August 25, 1976, Jacques Chirac resigned, the first prime minister to have done so under the Fifth Republic without having been asked to do so by the president. Giscard d'Estaing replaced him by Raymond Barre, a professor of economics and as non-political a figure, at the time, as Georges Pompidou had been in 1962. On December 5, 1976, Jacques Chirac founded the Rassemblement pour la République (RPR), with himself as president, with the result that when the next legislative elections were held, on March 13 and 19, 1978, there were two main right-wing parties competing for votes: the RPR and the Union pour la Démocratie Française (UDF), a federation of centre and non-Gaullist parties established only a short time before, on February 1, 1978.

In the event, the right won a narrow victory, rather to the surprise of the many commentators who had been predicting that the alliance between the socialists and the Communist Party would win power for the left for the first time since the establishment of the Fifth Republic in 1958. On June 26, 1972, the socialists and communists had signed the *Programme commun de la gauche*, and Giscard d'Estaing himself had been so impressed by the support for it that he had indicated, in a speech at Verdun-sur-le-Doubs on January 26, 1978, that he would feel obliged to appoint a government capable of putting the *programme commun* into action if the left won. However, the French Communist Party, probably under orders from Moscow, suddenly began, in late 1977, to devote far more time to attacking the socialists than criticising the very orthodox conservative economic policies being pursued by Raymond Barre, and the right was once again saved.

But if Giscard d'Estaing did not find himself faced after March 1978 with an Assemblée Nationale dominated by the left, his political troubles were by no means over. Since the Commune of 1871, Paris had been the only town in France not to have a mayor, being governed by a *préfet* appointed by the central government. A city with such a long tradition of revolutionary activity ought, it was felt, to be kept firmly in its place, and it was not until 1975 that the situation changed. Then, in December, and against the opposition of Jacques Chirac himself in the Assemblée Nationale, it was decided that Paris should have a mayor, and a bill was passed bringing Paris into line with the 36,000 other *communes*, with elections being held at the same time as in the rest of France, in March 1977. Not for the first or for the last time in his political career, Chirac changed his mind. On March 25, he stood against Giscard d'Estaing's candidate, Michel d'Ornano, and won. He thus became the first mayor of Paris, an influential and high profile post, which he was to hold until his election as president of the Republic in 1995.

On April 26, 1981 Chirac also decided to stand against Valéry Giscard d'Estaing, in the first round of the presidential elections. On the first round, he received 5,225,846 votes, which when added to the 8,222,432 cast for Giscard d'Estaing pointed to a France still generally well disposed to the right. There had been 7,505,960 for François Mitterrand, and 4,456,922 for the communist candidate Georges Marchais. The combined score of Giscard d'Estaing and Jacques Chirac was thus 13,448,278 as against 11,962,882 for Mitterrand and Marchais, and it is unlikely that many of those voting for Chirac would have supported a candidate from the left.

However, between the first and second ballot, Chirac rather pointedly refrained from urging the people who had voted for him to cast their votes for Giscard d'Estaing. All he said was that he personally could not vote for anyone else. Mitterrand won, making Giscard d'Estaing, at one and the same time, the first president of the Fifth Republic to complete the full seven-year term for which he had been elected by universal suffrage, as well as the first – and, so far, the only one – to be defeated when standing for re-election. In 1958, de Gaulle had been elected by an electoral college, and had resigned in April

1969 before completing the seven-year term for which he had been elected in 1965. Georges Pompidou died in office in April 1974, and François Mitterrand, as will be seen, served two full seven-year terms and was too ill as well as too old to exercise what would have been his constitutional right to stand for a third.

Although the behaviour of Jacques Chirac made an important contribution to Giscard d'Estaing's failure to be re-elected, there were other causes. Not only was he vulnerable to the accusation of being 'le Président du chômage' (the president of unemployment); because of the high profile which the Constitution of the Fifth Republic gave to the president, he was also held responsible for the fact that inflation had remained high, and that whereas he had inherited a favourable balance of payments, France now had a commercial deficit of 34 billion francs, and a budget deficit of 26 billion.

These were not, as the performance of the governments appointed by François Mitterrand after 1981 goes to show, problems that were easy to solve. All industrialised countries were affected by the crisis sparked off by the end of the monetary stability provided before August 1971 by the dollar, as well as by the increase in oil prices begun in 1973. France did not perform noticeably worse than other countries, and the various measures in favour of women and of equality between the sexes were not the only progressive reforms that Giscard d'Estaing helped to inspire.

Two million old age pensioners saw the purchasing power of their pension increase by 35 per cent between 1974 and 1980. The working week was reduced from 43 to 40 hours, and in 1980 a special allocation of 18,000 francs a year (£2,000 or $3,500) was created for the handicapped. By 1978, the lowest paid workers had received salary increases that were twice the average growth of earnings. In 1973, only one worker out of four was insured against unemployment. By 1978, the rate had risen to one in two, and workers made redundant through no fault of their own (*des licenciés économiques*) were guaranteed 90 per cent of their salary for the first year of unemployment.

Other social reforms, however well-inspired, attracted less universal approval. Traditionally-minded Catholics could scarcely be expected to vote for a president who had encouraged free contraception, helped to make divorce easier, and done nothing to resist the legalisation of abortion. The introduction of capital gains tax (*la taxation des plus-values*) had been one of the more specific issues on which Chirac and Giscard d'Estaing had not seen eye to eye, Giscard being for them and Chirac showing great reluctance to overcome the considerable right-wing opposition to them when the vote came to be taken in parliament. While Giscard d'Estaing's more conservative supporters were against the very idea of a capital gains tax, he was equally open to criticism from the left for not introducing the more easily understood and populist measure of a direct tax on capital.

In 1975, the Réforme Haby introduced the *collège unique*, the equivalent of the English comprehensive schools set up from 1966 onwards by the Labour government of Harold Wilson. The abolition of the system whereby children were divided at the age of eleven between those who were judged capable of benefitting from an academic education, and those who were not, proved as controversial in France as it was in England. Quality, it was argued, was being sacrificed for quantity, and Giscard d'Estaing again lost support among the traditionally-minded voters who were, according to his left-wing critics, his natural electorate.

Giscard d'Estaing had also made himself vulnerable to attacks from the right by his foreign policy. He was, and remains, an ardent European, and enjoyed an excellent relationship with the German Chancellor, Helmut Schmidt (1918–; Chancellor from 1974 to 1982). With the introduction, in March, 1979, of the European Monetary System, the two men co-operated in the first steps towards a single European currency, and it was Valéry Giscard d'Estaing's initiative which led, in December 1974, to the first of what became tri-annual meetings of the heads of state of what was then known as the European Community.

It was also Giscard d'Estaing who was a staunch supporter of the system whereby members of the European Parliament were elected by universal suffrage instead of being chosen from among members already elected to the parliaments of the member states, and the first of these elections took place in June 1979. But these moves towards greater European integration were not popular among neo-Gaullists, who regretted the apparent end of de Gaulle's insistence on *L'Europe des Patries*, especially when it was revealed that Giscard d'Estaing and Helmut Schmidt spoke to each other in English. This lent weight to the accusation made by Jacques Chirac in what was known as 'l'appel de Cochin', the statement which he issued from his hospital bed on September 13, 1978 after having been involved in a serious car accident.

The danger which he then stigmatised was that an increased influence of what he called 'le parti de l'étranger', a phrase which his audience could apply with equal ease to the Communist Party and its links with Moscow, to the growth of European federalism, as well as to the more insidious but equally disastrous penetration into

French life of Anglo-Saxon culture, with what the French see as its inevitable accompaniment of American economic and cultural imperialism. One of Jacques Chirac's proclaimed motives in creating the RPR, in December 1976, had been to fight against what he called 'la mainmise sur notre pays des tenants du collectivisme' (the increasing control of our country by supporters of collectivism). This, too, was a phrase intended to suggest that Giscard d'Estaing was far too moderate in his opposition to what is still known, in right-wing circles in France, as 'la coalition socialo-communiste', and some aspects of his behaviour on the international scene led credence to the view that he was 'soft on communism'.

On Christmas eve, 1979, Russian troops had moved into Afghanistan, ostensibly to support the Marxist government against its internal rivals. In the United States, as in Great Britain, the move was widely seen as yet another manifestation of Soviet imperialism, and vigorously condemned. France, however, refused to join its allies in the boycott of the 1980 Moscow Olympic games which other members of NATO tried to organise in protest, and in May 1980, Giscard d'Estaing went to Warsaw to meet the then Soviet leader, Leonid Brezhnev. It was not seen as a very sensible move, especially after the visit to Moscow in October 1975 in which he had taken part in a very elaborate ceremony of laying a wreath on Lenin's tomb, and earned for Giscard d'Estaing the condescending epithet from François Mitterrand of 'le petit télégraphiste de Moscou' (Moscow's little telegraph boy).

According to one school of thought, Chirac had a very clear plan in mind when he gave only luke-warm support to Giscard d'Estaing before the second ballot on May 10, 1981. He did, it is true, issue a series of very stern warnings against the dangers of allowing a socialist to come to power, pointing out that socialism had failed wherever it had been applied, and insisting on the dangers for France of any party which, like Mitterrand's socialists, was prepared to work with the communists. But he also, it has been suggested, thought that if Mitterrand were elected, the socialists would make such a mess of things that he would be called to power as the strong man capable of clearing up the mess.

If this is true, it is another example of Jacques Chirac's imperfect skills as a prophet, since François Mitterrand not only came to power but stayed there for fourteen years. His victory on May 10, 1981 by 1,065,956 of the votes cast in the second ballot of May 10, 1981, or 2.93 per cent of those voting, was also the result of a general feeling that it was time for a change in the politics of the Fifth Republic.

Giscard d'Estaing had also not helped his own cause by an indifference to public opinion surprising in so intelligent a man and explicable only by a mixture of hubris and what Baudelaire called 'le privilège aristocratique de déplaire' (the aristocratic pleasure of annoying people).

Although he is not particularly interested in eating any game which is shot, preferring scrambled eggs and smoked salmon, Giscard d'Estaing is a fanatical hunter. He naturally does not deign to turn his gun on plebeian animals such as rabbits or hares. But he is a great lad for slaughtering buffaloes, African elephants, lions, and African antelopes,[11] a passion which led him to be made an honorary citizen of Gabon, one of the countries in which he most frequently practised his favourite hobby. Indeed, the frequency with which Giscard d'Estaing's enthusiasm for big game hunting led him to be away from France inevitably led to a number of criticisms. The right-wing historian Pierre Gaxotte, writing in 1975 in *Le Spectacle du monde*, issued the reminder that 'la chasse a perdu Louis XVI' (hunting led to the ruin of Louis XVI), and said how unfortunate it would be, if there were serious trouble in France, and it turned out that the only way of contacting the president was by beating on the tom-tom.[12]

It was not, however, because he could not be reached in a crisis that Giscard d'Estaing's habit of spending long periods in Africa became one of the reasons for his failure to be re-elected in 1981. It was not even his passion for hunting. Most Frenchmen share his enthusiasm for killing wild animals, and probably admire him for being able to do so in such luxurious circumstances. It was because he had accepted a gift of some quite valuable diamonds from Jean Bedel Bokassa, Emperor of the Central African Republic.

The affair came to light, as most affairs do which are likely to cause embarrassment to French politicians, in the columns of *Le Canard enchaîné*. On October 10, 1979, shortly after Bokassa had been overthrown (on September 22) and gone into exile in the Ivory Coast, *Le Canard* published a photocopy of a document alleging that while he was minister of finance, in 1973, Giscard d'Estaing had received a plaquette of diamonds worth about a million francs from Bokassa, and that his cousins, François and Jacques, had been given similar presents. Jacques and François took *Le Canard* to court, and were awarded symbolic damages of one franc. Giscard d'Estaing took no action against the newspaper, but let it be known, on March 10, 1981, that he had paid a cheque of 40,000 francs to the central African Red Cross.

The affair naturally attracted a great deal of publicity, and was never satisfactorily cleared up. Giscard d'Estaing's supporters argued that the diamonds were far less valuable than *Le Canard enchaîné* alleged, and pointed out that General de Gaulle, whose reputation in financial matters was above reproach, had given house space at La Boisserie to a number of quite valuable presents which he had received as head of state. Since Giscard d'Estaing had been given the diamonds when he was minister of finance, and not head of state, this was not a particularly convincing reply. In particular, it fails to solve the problem of why Giscard d'Estaing, who had enough money of his own to buy as many diamonds as he liked, should have behaved in so extraordinary a fashion, and made himself so vulnerable over so eminently avoidable an issue.[13]

If the incident of the Bokassa diamonds was indeed a decisive factor in his losing the 1981 presidential election, it makes Giscard d'Estaing a member of a particular group of politicians: those who fell from grace through an error which was both minor and avoidable. Richard Nixon was well ahead in the presidential race of 1972, and had no need of any information which the break-in at the Watergate Hotel on June 17, 1972 might have brought him about the tactics likely to be followed by the Democratic Party. Cecil Parkinson (1932–), was on the way to becoming Mrs Thatcher's chosen successor as prime minister when he allowed himself to be embroiled in an adulterous affair. Jeffrey Archer (1940–) would have become chairman of the Conservative Party if he had not made himself vulnerable, quite unnecessarily in view of the immense wealth which he already possessed, to the suggestion of being somehow involved in insider dealing.

There is also a common feature to the twentieth-century politicians whose career ended in failure through what Hamlet calls 'the stamp of one defect', and which in his view brings particular men to ruin.[14] In the case of Nixon, it was a morbid suspicion of other people, in that of Cecil Parkinson, of straightforward lechery, for Jeffrey Archer, of a careless choice of friends, in the case of Giscard d'Estaing, of an aristocratic disdain for appearances. But in no case does the fate of the politicians who fail through a minor fault evoke either Hamlet's vision of the tragic fault, or Napoleon I's remark about tragedy nowadays lying in politics. It may well be, as is alleged in criticism of the attempt to study politics scientifically said to be characteristic of l'ÉNA, that the most fruitful lessons as to human behaviour are still to be found in Shakespeare and Machiavelli. But it is a salutary reminder of the difference between real politics in the twentieth century and the presentation of political action in imaginative literature, that men in lounge suits rarely attain the tragic dimension which hangs about those who wore a toga or doublet and hose.

4   François Mitterrand
The rebellious brother

Generalities

François Mitterrand was the first president of the Fifth Republic to
come to the office after his predecessor had completed the full seven-
year mandate for which he had been elected by universal suffrage. He
remains, at present, the only one to have completed two full terms in
office, as well as the only one to have been elected on a promise to
introduce fundamental changes in the social and economic structure of
France. He was the first to be obliged to appoint as prime minister a
politician from a party opposed to his own, thus acquiring the merit of
showing how flexibly the institutions of the Fifth Republic could be
made to work in practice. He thus gave reality to two relatively new
words in French political discourse: in 1981, that of *alternance*; and in
1986, that of *cohabitation*.

What Mitterrand's victory in the 1981 presidential election showed,
in this respect, was that the Constitution of the Fifth Republic was
not, as had been alleged, doomed always to give France a government
of the right. Power could move quite peaceably from right to left, just
as it had traditionally done in the English-speaking democracies which
regard such an event as so natural that they do not have a word such as
alternance to evoke the undisputed transfer of power from one political grouping to another after an election held under established rules
accepted by all parties.

In March 1986, when the Socialist Party lost the parliamentary elections, Mitterrand showed how the word *cohabitation* had also taken on
a new meaning. By appointing Jacques Chirac as prime minister, he
demonstrated how a left-wing president could govern quite peaceably,
if not always in total harmony, in tandem with a right-wing prime
minister. Between 1993 and 1995, he repeated the practice of *la cohabitation* with Édouard Balladur, again proving that the French no longer

believed that right and left were so incompatible that a practical co-operation between the two was impossible.

From 1958 onwards, Mitterrand had been violently opposed to the Constitution of the Fifth Republic, denouncing it as a virtual dictatorship, and basing much of his reputation on the virulence of his analysis in his 1964 pamphlet *Un Coup d'État Permanent*. It was, consequently, something of a surprise for his supporters to realise, when he left power in 1995, that this Constitution was if anything stronger than it had ever been. It is also unlikely that when he sought election as the first socialist president of the Fifth Republic, his supporters voted for him because they wanted a France in which the value of shares on the Stock Exchange was to rise by 500 per cent and the number of unemployed to increase from 1.5 million to almost 3 million. There is, in this respect, something of a similarity between him and de Gaulle. None of those who brought de Gaulle back to power in 1958 expected him to give Algeria its independence. Nobody who voted for Mitterrand did so because they thought he would reconcile the French Socialist Party with the market economy.

1916–81

François Mitterrand was born on October 26, 1916 at Jarnac, *le chef-lieu de canton* in the département de la Charente, in the west of France. Initially, his father worked for the Compagnie des Chemins de Fer Paris-Orléans, beginning his career by pushing trolleys along the station platform. After working his way up to the post of station master, he took early retirement in 1920 in order to devote himself to running the family vinegar-making business, ending up as president of the Fédération des fabricants de vinaigre de France.

Joseph Mitterrand followed his own beliefs, as well as local tradition in what is still a very conservative part of France, in having his children educated at Catholic schools, and was clearly faithful to the teachings of the Church on birth control. Mitterrand was the fifth in a family of eight children. When, however, on October 28, 1944, François Mitterrand married Danielle Gouze, he linked himself with the opposite tradition in France, that of an insistence on the secular nature of the French state. Although Mitterrand and his wife completed the civil ceremony required by law by a church service at St Séverin, they succeeded in limiting their family to three sons, Jean-Christophe, Gilbert and Pascal. Pascal died in infancy. Jean-Christophe and Gilbert both followed political careers, the elder as his father's adviser on African affairs, the younger as a socialist member, elected after his father had used his power as president to dissolve the National Assembly in 1981.

A major difference between Mitterrand and the four other presidents of the Fifth Republic became public knowledge in 1993, when it was revealed that he had an illegitimate daughter, Mazarine. Her mother, Anne Pigeot, with whom Mitterrand seems to have kept a separate household, was invited by Danielle Mitterrand to be present, with her daughter, at Mitterrand's funeral on January 9, 1996. De Gaulle and Pompidou had been model husbands and fathers, and if, as was occasionally alleged, Valéry Giscard d'Estaing had sometimes played away from home, it was with a discretion which Mitterrand seems to have lacked.[1]

Until 1925, Mitterrand was a boarder at the collège religieux d'Angoulême, where he stayed until taking his baccalauréat. In October 1936, at the age of 20, he followed the well-established tradition in France of going to Paris for his higher education. There, too, he remained linked with provincial Catholicism, just as François Mauriac had done almost thirty years earlier when he came up to Paris and stayed at the same student residence which Mitterrand's parents had chosen for him, Le Foyer des Pères Maristes, 104 rue Vaugirard. In 1954, in one of his 'Bloc Notes' for the then left-wing *L'Express*, Mauriac was to describe Mitterrand as being like the provincial hero in one of his own novels, and Mitterrand's early life does, like that of Georges Pompidou, follow the classic pattern of the young man coming up to Paris from the provinces to make his way in society which has been a stock theme in French literature from Balzac onwards.

Mitterrand followed another well-established tradition by studying both law and political science, and was not unusual in adopting the kind of right-wing attitudes later satirised by Jean-Paul Sartre in his 1939 story of a young fascist, 'L'Enfance d'un chef' ('Childhood of a Leader'), published in his 1939 collection *Le Mur* (*Intimacy*). The French right has always refused to recognise Jews as real Frenchmen, and there was a strongly anti-semitic element in the organisation which Mitterrand joined in 1936, the 'Volontaires Nationaux', the young helpers of 'les Croix-de-Feu' of Colonel François de la Roque (1885–1946).

Although theoretically devoted to protecting the interests of exservicemen, this was also a proto-fascist organisation, which resembled L'Action Française in being violently opposed to the Republic, and La Roque himself is credited with the invention of the slogan 'Travail,

Famille, Patrie' which the Vichy government used in 1940 to replace the republican 'Liberté, Égalité, Fraternité'.[2] La Roque himself, however, was not at all keen on the Vichy régime once it was established, and in 1943 was deported by the Germans. When taxed in later life with his earlier enthusiasm for right-wing politics, Mitterrand made the not unreasonable reply that it was much better for him to have travelled the way he had come instead of moving in the opposite direction.

Mitterrand fought courageously in the brief but disastrous campaign of 1940, was wounded and taken prisoner on June 14. On December 10, 1941, on his third attempt, he succeeded in escaping from his German prisoner of war camp, and made his way to Vichy. After the war, Mitterrand kept fairly quiet about the work which he then did for the Vichy régime. Although there were rumours even when he was at the height of his then uncontested fame, in 1981, nothing certain was known until 1994, when Patrice Péan published *Une Jeunesse française*. Indeed, on September 17, 1965, Mitterrand was reported in *Le Monde* as having denied ever receiving La Francisque, the decoration awarded by the Vichy government to its most faithful and effective servants. What Péan's book revealed was that Mitterrand had, between January and April 1942, worked at Vichy for a body called La Légion des combattants, one of whose slogans was 'Contre la lèpre juive, la pureté française' (Against Jewish leprosy, French purity).

In April 1942, Mitterrand was moved to the more congenial task of working for the Commissariat général des prisonniers de guerre. This work led him, in February 1943, to be officially received by Marshal Pétain, and to be decorated with La Francisque, the order which had, in 1940, replaced La Légion d'Honneur, and Péan insists that this was at his own request. Charles Maurras, the creator of L'Action Française and the man who had written of Léon Blum (1872–1950), the prime minister in the Popular Front government of 1936, that he was 'un homme à fusiller. Mais dans le dos' (a man to be shot. But in the back) had received Francisque number 2,202. Mitterrand's number was 2,068.

It was not a decoration that he ever recorded in his entry for *Who's Who in France*, and its possession would clearly have been an embarrassment for any Frenchman wishing to pursue a political career after 1944. There is nevertheless no reason to disbelieve his own explanation for accepting it: that by 1943, he was already involved in the resistance movement, and that a decoration from the Vichy régime was a good way of hiding this. It is also tempting to explain by personal rather than political reasons the fact that Mitterrand was not among the 47,000 or so recipients of the Médaille de la Résistance française. By the end of 1943, he had been sufficiently courageous in the resistance movement in occupied France, and proved successful enough, under the pseudonym of 'le capitaine Morland', in making a name for himself, to be summoned on December 2 to meet de Gaulle in Algiers.

De Gaulle began the conversation by criticising him for coming in a British aeroplane, before going on to insist on the need for all the resistance movements in France to accept his authority and his alone. This was not something which Mitterrand was prepared to do, and ready though Mitterrand was, as he wrote in *L'Express* in September 1987, to recognise de Gaulle as 'one of the greatest men in French history', he never accepted as either legal or legitimate the way de Gaulle had come back to power in 1958. The Gaullists, in return, did not see him as a man worthy to become president of the Republic. In May 1981, le Général de Boissieu, de Gaulle's son-in-law, resigned from his post as 'Grand Chancelier de la Légion d'Honneur' rather than fulfil what would otherwise have been his official duty of putting round Mitterrand's neck the 'collier du Grand Maître de l'Ordre' to which all presidents are officially entitled.

Mitterrand served briefly under de Gaulle immediately after the liberation, again with responsibility for prisoners of war and ex-servicemen. His subsequent career under the Fourth Republic, in which he served in eleven governments, was neither a dishonourable nor an untypical one. In 1950, as *ministre de la France d'outre-mer*, he encouraged the movement towards independence of the states of Black Africa. In September 1953, he resigned from the government of Joseph Laniel because he disagreed with its reluctance to grant independence to what was then French Morocco.

He did, in his capacity of ministre de l'intérieur in the government of the socialist Guy Mollet, greet the first attacks of the Front de Libération Nationale, on the night of October 31, 1954, with the statement that there could be no question of Algeria ever being anything but French, and that the police would soon put an end to the problem. But that was what virtually every politician continued to say until 1959. The publication in 1964 of *Un Coup d'État Permanent*, coupled with the inability of the socialists and communists to agree on a candidate, made him, in 1965, the obvious person to stand against de Gaulle in the first presidential contest based on universal suffrage since the election of Louis-Napoleon Bonaparte on December 10, 1848.

Mitterrand was generally seen as having done very well in preventing de Gaulle from being elected on the first ballot, on

December 5, 1965. He obtained 7,694,003 of the total of 24,254,554 votes cast, as against de Gaulle's 10,828,253. Only 15 per cent of those entitled to vote abstained, an indication that de Gaulle had judged the mood of the country correctly in 1962 when he changed the Constitution to make this possible.

The president of the Senate, Jean Lecanuet, with 3,777,119 votes, was supported by electors unhappy at de Gaulle's hostility towards further European unification as well as annoyed by his authoritarian style of government. Tixier-Vignancour, a well-known right-wing lawyer, probably drew most of his votes from people who thought that de Gaulle had been wrong to give Algeria its independence: 1,260,208, or 4.35 per cent of the total poll.

The student-led protest movement which had brought Paris to a standstill in 1968 did not show Mitterrand at his best. On May 28, he held a public meeting at which he proposed the establishment of a 'provisional government', headed either by himself or by Pierre Mendès France. It was not a very sensible suggestion, and it was only after he had been instrumental in founding the socialist party three years later at the Congrès d'Épinay, on December 11, 1971, that he began to be taken seriously again as a politician.

Rather curiously, in the light of the long tradition of left-wing politics in France, there had not been an actual socialist party making a serious bid for power since 1905, when the Parti socialiste français, established by Jean Jaurès (1859–1914) in 1901, had decided to call itself the Section Française de l'Internationale Ouvrière (SFIO). In 1921, after the Russian revolution of 1917, the SFIO had split between those who supported the Soviet Union, and who formed Le Parti Communiste Français, and the more moderate wing which kept the name SFIO and tended to ally itself for electoral purposes with the radicals.

François Mitterrand had never been a member of the SFIO, or indeed of any other grouping pursuing traditional socialist objectives. It is consequently a mark of how fully he had recovered both his skill as politician and his general reputation that he became, in December 1971, at one and the same time a member of the Socialist Party which he had just created and its first secretary. He then persuaded the Communist Party to sign a joint programme with the newly created Socialist Party on June 27, 1972.

The objectives of the 'Programme commun de gouvernment' included, in domestic politics, the nationalisation of all the key sectors of the French economy, a forty-hour working week, the strengthening of trade union rights, the guarantee that no old age pension would be less than 80 per cent of the basic wage established in 1970, the Salaire Minimum Interprofessionnel de Croissance (SMIC), the decentralisation of the administrative structure of the French state, and the absorption of private, Catholic schools into the state secular system. It also proposed the dissolution of NATO and the ending of France's independent nuclear deterrent.

Seen from the standpoint of the late 1990s, and especially of the performance of the British Labour Party under Tony Blair and the present French Socialist Party under Lionel Jospin, it has a curiously archaic air. It did, it is true, suggest an improvement in the French judicial system by proposing the introduction of habeas corpus, and proved sufficiently popular with the electorate to enable the left to do much better in the legislative elections of March 3 and March 10, 1973 than it had done in June 1968. After losing to de Gaulle in 1965, and with memories of his behaviour in May 1968 fresh in people's minds, Mitterrand had not stood against Pompidou in 1969. He thus made his second attempt when the right was divided between Giscard d'Estaing and Jacques Chirac, and almost won. After having come top in the first ballot, on May 5 1974, with 11,044,373 votes against Valéry Giscard d'Estaing's 8,326,774, and 3,857,728 for Jacques Chirac, he lost on the second ballot, on May 19, by a margin of 424,599 votes or 49.19 per cent of those voting, against 50.80 per cent. He received 12,971,604 votes against Giscard d'Estaing's 13,396,203. As in other presidential elections, the turn-out was high, with fewer than 13 per cent of those eligible to vote failing to do so.

Mitterrand's score in the 1974 presidential election showed that there was the potential for a left-wing victory, and a majority of candidates supporting the *programme commun* might have been elected in the legislative elections of March 1978 had it not been for a sudden change in the attitude of the French Communist Party. Although this was theoretically in alliance with François Mitterrand's Socialist Party, it suddenly began, in late 1977, to direct far more criticism at its supposed allies than at the fairly conservative government appointed by Giscard d'Estaing on August 27, 1976 under the leadership of Raymond Barre.

It almost certainly did this under directions from Moscow. In 1965, the USSR had made it clear that it supported de Gaulle rather than Mitterrand, and in 1974 it had also shown a similar preference for Giscard d'Estaing. The damage which a Gaullist or neo-Gaullist insistence on the need for France to remain independent of the United States might do to the foreign policy of the NATO alliance clearly outweighed, in Moscow's view, any advantages which the French working class might derive from a home-grown left-wing government.

It was this which led to the failure of the left to consolidate the gains which it had made in the first ballot, on March 12. Although the communist vote held steady, there was a general reluctance on the part of socialist voters to support candidates from the Parti Communiste Français, which they saw as having betrayed them by yet another change in the party line. The right saw its majority reduced, but the left did not win enough seats to form a majority. On April 5, 1978, Valéry Giscard d'Estaing was able to re-appoint Raymond Barre for his third period as prime minister, and François Mitterrand had another three years to wait before finally winning, at the age of 65, the power to put into practice the socialist ideas which he had begun to develop in the 1970s.

1981–4

With 14,642,306 votes over 15,708,262, or a lead of 1,065,956, in the second decisive round on May 10, 1981, Mitterrand's victory was less impressive than de Gaulle's lead of 2,463,964 over Mitterrand had been in 1965. This did not prevent it from giving rise to great public rejoicing, especially in Paris, when it was announced late in the evening of May 10, 1981. This euphoria was followed by a sufficiently serious panic the following day on the Stock Exchange to justify a twenty-four hour suspension of trading, and the process began whereby some of the less poverty-stricken members of the French middle classes filled the boot of their cars with bank notes and gold and headed for the Belgian or Swiss border. On May 21, Mitterrand officially took over the presidency, and did so in a more dramatic style than Giscard d'Estaing had adopted in 1974. There was a twenty-one gun salute, a visit to the Arc de Triomphe to lay a wreath on the Tomb of the Unknown Soldier, followed by an official lunch for 1,500 guests. In a carefully rehearsed television ceremony, Mitterrand then walked alone across la Place du Panthéon, carrying in his hand a rose, the symbol under which he and the Socialist Party had led his campaign.

The television cameras then followed him as he went alone into the crypt. There, to the accompaniment of Beethoven's 'Hymn to Joy', he laid a wreath on the tomb of Jean Jaurès, the founder in 1899 of the first French Socialist Party, as well as on that of Jean Moulin (1899–1943) the Resistance leader killed by the Germans, and of Victor Schoelcher (1804–93), 'Député de la Martinique et de la Guadeloupe', who on April 27, 1848 had given reality to at least one of the hopes of the February revolution by using his position as 'sous-secrétaire d'État à la marine' to put an end to slavery in the French colonies. An unkind journalist said that Mitterrand looked ill at ease during the ceremony, and compared him to a Belgian tourist looking for the loo.

Mitterrand appointed the socialist Pierre Mauroy (1928–) to the office of prime minister. It was a novelty not only in the politics of the Fifth Republic, where no left-wing politician had held this office since its foundation in 1958, but also in Mauroy's professional origins. Like Georges Pompidou, he was *un fils d'instituteur*, the son of a primary school teacher. But unlike the previous six prime ministers of the Fifth Republic, he had never been a senior member of the civil service.[3] He had, it is true, as a member of the Corps de l'Éducation Nationale, at one time been a civil servant, but only at the humble level of teacher of technical subjects. He had, moreover, left teaching fairly early, having become a trade union official after only three years in the classroom, before going on to a career in local government. In 1971, he had been elected mayor of Lille, and from 1973 onwards had illustrated the meaning of the term *le cumul des mandats* by combining this with a seat as député for a Lille constituency.

Mauroy's government nevertheless contained eight former pupils of the École Nationale d'Administration, with two of the posts as ministre d'État going to Michel Rocard, a member of the Inspection des Finances in charge of *l'aménagement du territoire* (land usage and development), and to Jean-Pierre Chevènement, another *énarque*, responsible for research and development. However, while 90 per cent of the presidential staff under de Gaulle had been civil servants, and 89 per cent under Giscard d'Estaing, the proportion fell under Mitterrand to 40 per cent. He preferred, as Alistair Cole puts it in his admirable *François Mitterrand: A Study in Political Leadership*, to surround himself with 'writers, artists, party loyalists and university professors'.[4]

On May 22, 1981 Mitterrand used the power given to him by Article 12 of the Constitution to dissolve the Assemblée Nationale first elected in March 1978, and which in theory therefore still had another two years to run. In the legislative elections of June 14 and June 21, 1981, the Socialist Party obtained an absolute majority of 33 over all other parties, including the communists. On the public relations front, as well as on that of parliamentary arithmetic, this was one of Mitterrand's greatest triumphs. For the first time in France, a left-wing party could exercise power without being beholden to the communists. Mitterrand's decision to keep on as ministers the four communists originally appointed on May 21, 1981, immediately after he had taken over the presidency, thus became more a gesture of condescending tolerance than a promise to do what the communists might suggest.

The socialists were now in power, though one of their députés, André Laignel, put it rather strongly when he said to his parliamentary colleagues sitting on the right of the Chamber, 'Vous avez juridiquement tort parce que vous êtes politiquement minoritaires' (You are legally in the wrong because you are in a political minority). For all Mitterrand's earlier criticism of them, the institutions of the Fifth Republic had shown themselves just as able to give power to the left as to the right. Although not an event which Charles de Gaulle would have predicted, it was fully in the logic of the institutions which he had created. *L'alternance*, a word which de Gaulle would have known only as applied to electric current, had worked at the parliamentary level as well as on that of the presidency. Mitterrand had a clear five years to put the 110 propositions on which he and his party had fought both elections into practice, and he himself had been elected for seven years.

Like Giscard d'Estaing, Mitterrand was more successful as a reformer on the social than on the economic front. August 8, 1981, saw the abolition of the Cour de Sûreté de l'État, the special court set up to judge what the government chose to consider as political crimes. Henceforth, as in other countries following the Western democratic tradition, the category of political crime ceased to exist in France. Although the fear of jury intimidation has led to the creation of a special court, consisting of seven professional judges, to judge terrorist offences, anyone accused of killing or stealing for political reasons is judged by the same criteria as those applied to criminals inspired by private motives.

An even more important change was made on November 11, 1981, when the Assemblée Nationale voted to abolish the death penalty. It was a decision which brought France into line with other European countries. It was a humane decision, but of a type which might have been carried out by a government headed by Giscard d'Estaing. The same is true of the disappearance, in August 1981, of the state monopoly on broadcasting, and the inclusion of Article 1 of the law of July 2, 1982 declaring that 'Les citoyens ont droit à une communication audiovisuelle libre et pluraliste' (Citizens have the right to a television system which is free of government control and expresses all points of view).

It was in its readiness to reduce the power of the state over its citizens that Mitterrand's policies differed most sharply from the socialism imposed on the citizens of Eastern Europe by the armies of the Soviet Union, just as it was in the continued attempt to improve the position of women that he and his followers differed from traditional French conservatism.

In 1981, a special ministry was established to promote the rights of women, and on July 13, 1982, a bill was passed imposing on all employers the duty to provide equal pay for equal work, and in 1985 the traditional right of the husband to decide on the financial affairs of the household was replaced by an equal partnership between man and wife. On December 31, 1982, it became possible for a woman deciding to have a voluntary termination of pregnancy to have the cost of the operation and her stay in hospital repaid by the social security system.

In December 1981, the 'lois Auroux' greatly improved the position of trade unions, requiring employers to negotiate annual increases of salary, and to recognise unions as partners in deciding working conditions. The position of employees was also improved by the implementation of the promise to reduce the length of the working week from forty to thirty-nine hours, with no reduction in salary, to increase compulsory holidays with pay from four to five weeks a year, and to raise the compulsory minimum wage, the Salaire Minimum Interprofessionnel de Croissance, by 10 per cent.

Like other measures taken in the early years of Pierre Mauroy's premiership, and which represented what Mitterrand wanted to do as distinct from what he was obliged to do later, this increase was inspired as much by a particular economic theory as by a concern for social justice. Like the increase of 25 per cent in family allowances and of 15 per cent in old age pensions, the reduction of the retirement age to 60, and like the immediate creation of 54,000 new jobs in the public sector and a proposed increase to 400,000 in 1983, it was intended to reduce unemployment.

Unemployment had now reached 1,700,000, and the new government took the view propagated by J. Maynard Keynes (1883–1946) in the 1930s. This theory explained the persistence of unemployment by the tendency of capitalism to produce more goods than the low wages paid to the workers could enable them to buy. It was therefore the duty of governments to make up for this shortage by stimulating demand, if necessary by what Keynes's supporters called deficit financing and his opponents described in less flattering terms as printing money.

The Mauroy government of 1981 also took the view that the state could manage the national economy better than could private enterprise. It therefore undertook an ambitious programme of nationalisation, taking under public control the whole of the steel industry, as well as the glass-making firm of Saint Gobain, the electronics giant Thompson-Brandt, Rhône-Poulenc, the armament manufacturer Matra, and thirty-six major banks as well as the financial houses of Paribas and Suez. Only the state, it was argued, could use the credit provided by banks efficiently, just as only the state could ensure the continued financial independence of France by protecting its major industrial concerns against foreign take-overs.

French socialism of the 1980s also differed from the type practised by the countries under Soviet control by providing adequate compensation for former share-holders. As an article in *Le Monde* on September 9, 1991 pointed out, the French state was paying almost 25 per cent above the genuine market price. By the end of 1983, when the nationalisation programme was completed, it was calculated that it had cost each household in France some 3,250 francs, or the equivalent of £300 or US$550. Some of the nationalised industries saw their profits increased, so much so that when, in 1986, the conservative government of Jacques Chirac decided to privatise them, they proved highly attractive to private investors. CGE, Saint Gobain, Péchiney, Rhône-Poulenc, Thompson and Bull all changed from a position where they were either making a loss or just managing to balance their books, to the point where they made quite healthy profits, and supporters of increased state control of the economy point out that the U-turn carried out after 1986 came too early to allow the policy of nationalisation to achieve its full potential.

These policies nevertheless failed in two respects: the increase in purchasing power created by the reflation policy (*la politique de relance*) of 1981–3 did not bring about a decrease in unemployment; and the fall in the value of the franc on the international markets obliged the government to change its policy. On June 10, 1982, it introduced a policy of price control and wage restraint, and on January 30, 1983, the trade union leader Edmund Maire, whose Confédération Française des Travailleurs had been one of the main supporters of Mitterrand's brand of socialism, made a joint announcement with the president of the need to introduce *la politique de rigueur*, a policy of restraint both in wage increases and government expenditure.

The increase in purchasing power in France had not led to a revival of French industry. It had produced, instead, so large an increase in imports in order to satisfy demand that the franc had to be revalued on three separate occasions in the European Monetary System: by 3 per cent on October 4, 1981; by 5.5 per cent on June 12 1982; and by 2.5 per cent on March 21, 1983. Each of these devaluations had been accompanied by an increase in what was also known as the European Exchange Rate Mechanism both of the Deutschmark and of the Dutch guilder, so that after less than two years of socialism, the French franc had lost some 15 per cent of its purchasing power on the international market.

The franc might, in March 1983, have fallen even further if Mitterrand had not then taken a decision which illustrates at one and the same time the nature of the power which the president has under the Fifth Republic, and the essentially pragmatic nature of his own socialism. Membership of the EMS had always been essentially voluntary. It was thus different from the European Common Currency due to be introduced on January 1, 1999, in that a country could always decided to leave it, and let its currency float, if this was thought to be economically advantageous.

This was what the United Kingdom was to do on September 16, 1992, and which the Mauroy government could have done in March 1983. However, Mitterrand personally intervened in the debate in order to ensure that the franc stayed within the European Monetary System, with everything which this implied by way of maintaining its revised parity with the German mark and observing a much tighter monetary policy. There was, in other words, to be an end to Keynesianism in France, together with the adoption of the same kind of strict control over public expenditure which had, since May 1979, characterised British economic policy under Margaret Thatcher, and, since 1980, the policy followed by the United States under Ronald Reagan.

It was unlucky both for Mitterrand himself and for French socialism that he should have come to power in 1981, just as it had been unlucky for Léon Blum that the government of the Popular Front should have been elected in May 1936. Blum's expansionist policies were thrown off course by the need to devote more resources to rearmament. Mitterrand's government was unable to pursue its programme of reflation and of increasing the purchasing power of the average French citizen by international conditions over which he had no control. With every other industrialised country trying to limit the purchasing power of its citizens, the seller's market created by the *politique de relance* drew imports into France like a suddenly opened window drawing cold air into an over-heated house.

A major factor here, as in the problems faced by Giscard d'Estaing's government, was the price of oil. This had begun to fall on the international markets, thanks partly to the inventiveness of Western technology in finding new sources not under the control of OPEC (the

Organization of Petroleum-Exporting Countries), and partly by the realisation by these countries that if they did succeed in their apparent aim of destroying Western capitalism, they would kill the goose which gave them their golden eggs. It was nevertheless not a reduction which brought any particular benefit to France, a country which had virtually no oil resources of its own, and therefore had to buy it on the international market, where it was priced in dollars.

The policies adopted by the Reagan administration, coupled with the absence of a rival currency to the dollar offering a relatively safe haven at a time of continuing inflation, caused the value of the United States dollar to rise from 4.5 francs in 1980 to 5.4 in May 1982, and then to 8.2 in 1984 before peaking at 9.36 in June 1985. If the purchase of oil was not to become completely impossible, the French government had to pursue a policy which protected the value of the franc. This it could do, in a world in which all the other major industrial powers were adopting deflationary policies, only by following their example. The attempt to achieve economic growth by a Keynesian style pump-priming, together with the attempt to improve living standards for the less fortunate members of society, had to be sacrificed to the need for a balanced budget and a strong currency.

It was an early example of what, in the 1990s, has come to be known as globalisation. The abolition of customs duties between what were then the ten members of the European Economic Community (France, Italy, Belgium, the Federal Republic of Germany, Italy, the United Kingdom, Ireland, Luxembourg, Holland and Greece) made it impossible for France to protect her industries against European competition. If her citizens wanted to use the increased purchasing power given to them by the *politique de relance* to buy German cars or Italian shoes, there was nothing that any government, whether of the right or the left, could do about it. The president of the Fifth Republic might, in theory and in terms of French internal politics, have more power at his disposal than either the British prime minister or the president of the United States. But he could not use this power to follow an economic policy which world circumstances made highly dangerous for the over-all prosperity of his country.

De Gaulle has the advantage, in any comparison with Mitterrand, of never having said in advance what policy he would follow in Algeria. He could therefore quite easily betray the people who had brought him back to power in 1958 without being accused of going back on his word. There is no equivalent in the *110 Propositions pour la France* on which Mitterrand had been elected in 1981 to the irony in de Gaulle's 'Algériens, je vous ai compris' speech of July 1958.

Mitterrand had quite clearly promised a policy of reflation and nation-alisation, which he was now having to abandon.

The readjustment of the value of the franc on March 21, 1983, enabled France to remain within the European Monetary System. But it had been accompanied by the adoption of a further *plan de rigueur* symbolised by the introduction of exchange controls and the imposi-tion of a forced loan of 1 per cent on all taxable income. France had also, by linking the franc to the value of the mark, confirmed the strength of the link with Germany first established by de Gaulle in 1961. But what was to become known as the policy of *le franc fort* also meant the end of traditional socialism in France. Since the economy of the Federal Republic of Germany was firmly based on a strongly monetarist version of capitalism, with everything which a banker's agenda implies by way of the sacrifice of generous social policies to sound money, the French economy had to follow the same path.

1984–8

Number 90 of the *110 Propositions pour la France* on which Mitterrand had been elected in 1981 promised to offer further support for the traditional socialist idea of excluding religious instruction from the syllabus of all schools. It announced this intention, in the rather coded language characteristic of debates on this topic in France, by calling for the establishment of 'un grand service public laïque et unifié de l'éducation nationale'. What the phrase actually meant for French socialists, if not for Mitterrand himself, was that private schools, of which 92 per cent are Catholic, would have to make a choice: either they would have to decide, as the direct grant schools in England have had to decide, between becoming completely independent, with every-thing that this meant by way of meeting all their costs; or they would have to accept integration into the state system, based as it is in France on strictly secular principles. Since the 'loi Debré' of 1959, which had seemed to confirm the essentially right-wing nature of de Gaulle's government by giving them fairly generous subsidies, they had been largely independent of the state-run, secular system. This was now going to have to change.

In 1984, after two years of negotiation between Alain Savary, the education minister, and the Catholic school authorities, the govern-ment introduced a bill aimed at implementing Proposition 90, and accepted a number of amendments put forward by the socialist majority in the Assemblée Nationale. The Catholic hierarchy had no problems in reading the code, but had a slightly different set of priorities from the powerful UNAPEL (Union des parents d'élèves de l'école libre – the Association of parents of children in non-secular schools).

What the hierarchy was concerned with was maintaining the specific identity of Catholic schools. What was of greater interest to many members of the UNAPEL was the possibility of continuing to send their children to privately-run schools, with their higher standards, smaller classes, better discipline and better teachers, and of doing so, as the 'loi Debré' had allowed, largely at the tax-payer's expense.

All schools in France, if the *projet Savary* went through, would effectively be absorbed into the state system. Children would be required to attend the establishment designated by the authorities. Both school heads and classroom teachers would be appointed by the ministry, as in the state system. It was not an idea which appealed to the class in which Mitterrand had been born and brought up, and the widespread demonstrations against it culminated in a meeting at Versailles on March 3, 1984 attended by 800,000 people, followed by one in Paris on June 24 which was said by its organisers to have brought together over a million.

On July 12, however, Mitterrand suddenly announced that the *projet Savary* was to be withdrawn. Several days earlier, he had said publicly 'J'entends rester fidèle à mes engagements, mais je tiens compte de plus en plus de ces millions qui pensent autrement que moi' (I intend to keep my promises, but more and more I am bearing in mind the millions of French men and women who do not share my views). When, however, he suddenly announced that the bill was to be withdrawn, he did so without consulting any of the ministers concerned. Savary himself learned that his law was not to go through by watching a television news broadcast, and immediately resigned. He was followed on July 17 by the prime minister, Pierre Mauroy.

Mitterrand had shown that however limited his powers might be in an economic context, he was still master of what happened in the narrower field of French internal politics, and the symbolism of his decision was perhaps just as important as the way in which it was announced. Support for a wholly secular system of education, accompanied by a reluctance to see the tax-payer's money used to support Catholic schools, had been a hallmark of French socialism since its very beginning in the early nineteenth century. By abandoning it, and creating a situation where 'les écoles libres' remained free of state control, Mitterrand was confirming that this aspect of the socialism of the nineteenth and early twentieth centuries belonged to a past which could not be revived.

Subsequent agreements between the government and the Catholic school authorities laid down the conditions under which subsidies could be given, and under which teachers in 'les écoles libres' would be trained and recruited. As a teacher in one of these schools later commented to me, in 1997, 'c'est tout de même extraordinaire que ce soit les socialistes qui ont permis la titularisation des enseignants du privé' (it's extraordinary all the same that it should have been the socialists who have enabled teachers in church schools to have security of tenure).

From another point of view, however, the way the *projet Savary* was withdrawn is something of an indictment of the political system of the Fifth Republic. It is not normal, in an established parliamentary democracy, for one man, however democratically elected, to have the power to take a decision of this kind without any consultation with his colleagues. It is also a poor reflection on French political culture in general that the only way of defeating a measure likely to affect the lives of millions of people is by mass demonstrations, with everything they imply by way of a threat to public order.

In a more encouraging vein, and one which suggests a further similarity between Mitterrand and de Gaulle, the decision to withdraw the *projet Savary* is another example of a government being elected to apply one policy and then doing the exact opposite. Just as it is hard to imagine a left-wing politician successfully giving up the policy of L'Algérie Française, it is equally improbable that any government of the right would have got away with a policy of such blatant favouritism to private schools. At no time since the establishment of the Third Republic in 1870 has the situation of Catholic schools looked more secure; except, perhaps, between 1940 and 1944. At no time in history has a socialist party given the French middle class the opportunity of requiring the general tax-payer to finance a system of education which places its children in so favourable a position, especially at the crucial age of 11 to 16.

On July 19, 1984, Mitterrand appointed Laurent Fabius, a member of the Conseil d'État, and, at 37, the youngest man to serve as prime minister in twentieth-century France. He was the second *énarque* to be appointed to the post – Jacques Chirac had been the first, when he served between 1974 and 1976 under Giscard d'Estaing – and was clearly readier than Mauroy to carry out the kind of economic policy which Mitterrand had already defined at a press conference on February 4, 1984, when he said that the only viable source of investments for any economy were the profits made by firms run on commercial principles. The government then proceeded to show what this meant by announcing that in order to conform to EEC regulations banning subsidies to competitive industries, the steel industry would be rationalised and made profitable by reducing the number of people it employed.

By this time, there was little to surprise Mitterrand's critics on the left, especially since the priority given to keeping the franc within the European Monetary System had been paralleled by a general attitude in foreign affairs which made Mitterrand seem more of a Cold War warrior than any of his three predecessors had been. Once the Soviet Union had decided, in the early 1950s, to change its policy from support for Israel to providing arms for the Arab states seeking to destroy her, it had become an article of faith on the left that Israel was an aggressive, imperialist power whose main function was to enable the United States to spread its influence in the Middle East.

When, therefore, on March 3, 1982, Mitterrand became the first president of the Fifth Republic to visit Israel, his action was not only seen as a break with the tradition in foreign policy expressed by de Gaulle's 1967 description of the Jews as 'un peuple d'élite, sûr de lui et dominateur'. It was also interpreted as another conscious act of defiance of the left, and especially of the Communist Party, still obediently following the policy of hostility to Israel adopted by the Soviet Union in the 1950s. On March 4, in his speech to the Knesset, Mitterrand made the recognition of the right of Israel to exist a precondition of the establishment of a Palestinian state. Later, when Yasser Arafat gave a speech on May 2, 1989 declaring that the original charter of the Palestine Liberation Organization demanding the destruction of the State of Israel was now 'out of date', French historians see it as more than a mere coincidence that he did so in Paris.

Mitterrand also took what was seen as an even more right-wing stance on the major problem of defence policy to dominate the 1980s. This was the question of whether or not the NATO alliance should install Cruise and Pershing missiles in Western Europe in response to the deployment by the Soviet Union, from the mid-1970s onwards, of the SS20 missiles on the territory of its allies in the Warsaw Pact. The novelty of the SS20s, and their advantage from the point of view of the Soviet Union, lay in their accuracy. Earlier missiles had been so inaccurate that they could destroy a specific target in Western Europe such as an aerodrome or missile site only if they contained so large a nuclear charge that the fall out, carried by the prevailing west–east winds, would do almost as much damage to the Soviet Union as to the inhabitants of Germany, Italy or Holland. The SS20s, in comparison, were capable of landing so close to their target that it had become technically possible for the Soviet Union to wipe out all the American bases in Western Europe in one surprise attack. The United States would then have no choice between abandoning its allies or retaliating by an attack against the cities of the Soviet Union, which would bring about the total destruction of both countries.

On January 20, 1983, Mitterrand visited the Federal Republic of Germany, and gave a speech to the Bundestag in which he commented, with some accuracy, that 'the pacifists are in the West but the missiles in the East'. It was, as critics unenthusiastic about French defence policy in general pointed out, an attitude which it was relatively easy for him to take. Since de Gaulle's decision in March 1966 to withdraw French forces from the NATO command structure, while still remaining a member of the alliance, there had been no American bases on French soil. Mitterrand's speech to the Bundestag did not therefore imply that France was going to accept the missiles herself. However, since the French had learned between 1940 and 1944 what it was like to be occupied by a totalitarian power, there were no protest movements comparable to those organised in the United Kingdom round the bases at Greenham Common and elsewhere.

It is one of the paradoxes of French politics that Mitterrand's policy towards the Soviet Union should have been so much harder than that of politicians theoretically further to the right, such as Giscard d'Estaing and Pompidou. It involved the abandonment of the statement in the *110 Propositions pour la France* to the effect that France was 'more threatened by capitalism than by the USSR', just as the support which he gave to the United Kingdom in 1982 at the time of the Falklands War involved a temporary jettisoning of de Gaulle's hostility towards what he always called 'les Anglo-Saxons', as well as of his attempt to win friends in Latin America. But if Mitterrand's behaviour towards dictatorships, of the left as of the right, showed the same grasp of realpolitik which had inspired John Kennedy in 1962, and which was to govern the behaviour of Thatcher and Reagan in the 1980s, he was shown to less advantage by what one hopes was the unauthorised behaviour in the Pacific by some of his more zealous subordinates.

On July 10, 1985, agents from the French Secret Service found their way into Auckland Harbour and blew up the *Rainbow Warrior*, a ship belonging to the Greenpeace movement which was preparing to protest against the holding of French nuclear tests in the Pacific. An Italian photographer, Fernando Pereira, was killed, and there was no serious attempt to deny that the two members of the Direction Générale de la Sécurité Extérieure (DGSE) arrested by the New Zealand police on July 12 were guilty of what it would be charitable but misleading to describe as manslaughter. In the end, neither of them suffered more than a few months in a New Zealand prison, followed by three years on the French atoll of Hao.

The French government, having shown what damage it could do to the New Zealand economy by an insistence on every detail of the regulations governing the import into the EEC of New Zealand butter and lamb, eventually apologised and paid 50 million francs damages. In France itself, the public outcry led eventually to the resignation of the defence minister, Charles Hernu, who was widely seen as having been sacrificed to save not only the prime minister, Laurent Fabius, but the president himself. It was convincingly argued that Mitterrand had either been culpably ill-informed when he denied all knowledge of the affair, or was being deliberately dishonest, and the scandal of the *Rainbow Warrior* showed France in the unfortunate role of both bully and blackmailer.

By the time the next legislative elections were due to be held, on March 16, 1986, the Socialist Party had been in power for almost five years, and public opinion polls showed it to have lost so much support that its only hope of avoiding a catastrophic defeat lay in changing the rules of the game. Mitterrand and Fabius consequently decided, on June 26, 1985, to implement proposition number 47 of the *110 Propositions pour la France* announced in the *projet Socialiste* of 1980 and replace the *scrutin uninominal à deux tours* by a system based on proportional representation.

This did not save the Socialist Party from losing the election, and on March 20, 1986, only three days after the announcement of the results, Mitterrand announced that he was appointing Jacques Chirac as prime minister. The composition of the Chirac government was announced the same evening. There was no place in it for Giscard d'Estaing, who would apparently not have been unhappy to have been invited to serve as prime minister, but whose party, the Union pour la Démocratie Française (UDF), had won only 53 seats as against 76 for Chirac's Rassemblement pour la République (RPR).

The Communist Party was down from 42 to 35, exactly the same number which Jean-Marie Le Pen's Front National had been able to win by the introduction of the proportional representation system. The fact that an overtly racist party had, for the first time under the Fifth Republic, won seats in the Assemblée Nationale, was an ironic comment on the first five years of a period in which the left had held undisputed political power, as well as a key to the main reason for the Socialist Party's defeat: the fact that unemployment, already at the 1.6 million mark in 1981, had risen to 2.5 million, or over 10 per cent of the population, by 1986. The reflationary policies adopted in 1981 had not worked, and the adoption from July 1982 onwards of a series of austerity measures had led to the feeling that for the poor and the unemployed, there was little to choose between right and left.

But although the *New York Times* for March 2, 1986 had given quite a favourable verdict on the first five years of Mitterrand's presidency, the loss in value of the franc, coupled with what was now being revealed about the high cost of the nationalisation programme, strengthened the impression that the French Socialist Party, like the British Labour Party of Harold Wilson in the 1960s and mid-1970s, had won power on a series of promises to improve the economy of the country, which it had not been able to keep.

The result was that the governments of Pierre Mauroy and Laurent Fabius were not given credit for what they had achieved in a more general context. Mitterrand had promised that the decentralisation of French local and regional government would be 'la grande affaire du Septennat' and the laws passed on February 2, 1982 and January 7, 1983 did enable locally elected representatives to have more say in the running of their area. Since the time of the first Napoleon, the rule known as *la tutelle préfectorale* had insisted that all decisions involving public expenditure taken by locally elected bodies needed the approval of the centrally appointed *préfet*. This was now abolished, and the *préfet* himself given the new title of *commissaire de la République*, before resuming his original title in 1987.

But this transfer of decision making from Paris to the provinces was inevitably accompanied by an increase in local taxation. The amount spent by local authorities rose from 4.5 per cent to over 6 per cent of the Gross National Product, but with no corresponding decline in the taxes levied nationally. Decentralisation was also, for the average voter, a relatively technical matter whose financial and practical advantages, if any, would be slow in coming. The earlier reforms such as the abolition of the death penalty, the measures in favour of equality between the sexes and the increased freedom of the mass media from government control, now dated from so long ago that they were taken for granted, and weighed little by the side of the continued rise of unemployment and the increase in insecurity and petty crime.[5]

When, on April 4, 1986, Jacques Chirac took his first vote of confidence in the Chambre des Députés, he had a majority of 292 to 285. Narrow though the margin was, it emphasised how inevitable the practice of *la cohabitation* had become. Mitterrand still had the power of dissolving the newly elected Assemblée Nationale and asking the country to think again. He preferred, however, to hold his power of dissolution over the head of the government as a permanent threat. He knew that there were only two years to go before another presidential election gave him the chance of a renewed mandate, with everything that this implied for a dissolution from a position of strength. He also had enough confidence in his own ability as a vastly more experienced politician to outplay Jacques Chirac at the public relations game, and thus make his own re-election in 1988 more certain.

The result of the legislative election of March 16, 1986 was a reminder that the Fifth Republic, for all the formal powers vested in the president, was a parliamentary democracy in the sense that the government could raise money only by raising taxes agreed by a freely elected legislative assembly. Like the president of the United States, the president of the Fifth Republic has no tax-raising powers, and no authority to make laws. If the elected assembly decides to assert its authority in the way which defines a parliamentary democracy, that of withholding supply, there is no way in which the president can govern the country.

In the case of the Fifth Republic, there is also remarkably little that the president can do to stop a bill from becoming law once it has been approved by parliament. He can, according to Article 10, ask parliament to think again, and parliament cannot refuse, so long as he does so within fifteen days of its original vote. But there is no stipulation comparable to the rule in the United States which says that the presidential veto can be over-ridden only if Congress votes against him by a two-thirds majority. The implication is that, as Churchill once put it, 'one is enough', so that even a government with a very narrow majority can require the president to exercise the duty given to him by Article 10 of the 1958 Constitution of promulgating the laws which parliament has passed.

The election of March 1986 had been dominated by what has become, since the rise of socialism in the nineteenth century, and more especially since the 1920s, the defining issue separating right from left: is the economy of the country best run by capitalism, that is to say by private firms seeking to maximise profits for their shareholders? Or is it more efficient, as well as a better way of ensuring social justice, to choose the socialist method of entrusting the process of wealth creation to publicly owned corporations which are able to follow a nationally defined plan and give priority to the interests of the community at large?

In May and June 1981, Mitterrand had won the presidential election, and the Socialist Party the legislative elections, by persuading the electorate that it was better to choose the second way. In 1986, the right-wing coalition of the UDF and the RPR had won electoral support for the capitalist rather than for the socialist alternative. Although they had a narrower majority than the Socialist Party enjoyed in 1981, it was one which entitled them to put their policies into action, and there was, as long as they played their cards right, nothing that the president could do to stop them. And just as Margaret Thatcher had done in the Great Britain of the 1980s, Jacques Chirac's government introduced a programme of privatisation. Companies which had earlier been taken into public ownership were to be returned to the private sector, and shares in them put on sale on the Stock Exchange.

Initially, the Chirac government of April 1986 tried to do this by using Article 38 of the Constitution, which enables the law to be changed by decrees approved in Cabinet ('ordonnances et décrets délibérés en Conseil des Ministres'), without going through parliament. However, on the highly symbolic date of July 14, 1986, in the television address which the president traditionally makes on the anniversary of the fall of the Bastille, Mitterrand announced that he would not sign the decrees, and told the government that they would have to bring a law before parliament. Article 34 of the Constitution of the Fifth Republic lays down those areas in which the rules governing the organisation of the state and the economy are determined by laws. These include not only civil rights, the raising of taxes, the way in which elections are held, but also what it calls 'les nationalisations d'entreprises et les transferts de propriété d'enterprises du secteur public au secteur privé' (nationalisation of firms and the transfer of property of firms from the public to the private sector). There was therefore no real constitutional obstacle to the Chirac government bringing in its privatisation programme, but Mitterrand had made it just that little bit more difficult, while at the same time reminding the electorate of his existence.

The word 'privatisation' was a relatively new one, having more positive connotations than denationalisation, and section 3 of paragraph 49 places all Fifth Republic governments in a very strong position in their relationship with parliament. It states that any motion of no-confidence must be signed by at least one-tenth of the membership of the Assemblée Nationale, and that a full forty-eight hours must elapse between its presentation and any vote on it. It also lays down that only those députés actually voting against the government have their votes counted. All other members of the Assemblée Nationale, whether they have taken a conscious decision to abstain or are merely not there, are deemed to have voted in favour of the government. Paragraph 3 of

Article 49, also gives the government the power to make any bill a question of confidence, and the same rules apply. Unless there is a positive majority against the government, the bill is automatically passed.

The left did not command a sufficient majority to prevent the privatisation bill from going through, and Mitterrand had no choice, during the last two years of his first term as president, but to watch the banks and industries nationalised between 1981 and 1986 returned to private ownership. But he had gained the tactical advantage of placing Chirac in a position where he had to have recourse to Article 49.3, and therefore to look like something of a bully. In the meantime, he had used his power to refuse to sign decrees in order to look like the guardian of democracy and of the public interest. It was a tactic that he was to use again, and which is one of the factors which help to explain why he won a second term as president in May 1988.

There was enough money around in the community at large to make what Harold Macmillan called the 'selling off of the family silver' – a term which the French translate as 'la vente des bijoux de famille' – as much of a success in the France of François Mitterrand and Jacques Chirac as it had been only a few years earlier in the England of Margaret Thatcher. The sale of Saint-Gobain, the first of the enterprises to be sold off, in December 1986, was particularly successful, and since the steel-making firms of Usinor and Sacilor had also been made highly profitable by the cost-cutting policies of Laurent Fabius, they too were highly attractive to investors.

Although 63 per cent of those questioned in a public opinion poll early in 1985 had said that they would prefer the forthcoming parliamentary election to produce a situation where the president and the prime minister belonged to the same party, *la cohabitation* was quite popular. Mitterrand played a weak hand very skilfully, taking the opportunity once again in December 1986 to refuse to sign a decree on the redrawing of electoral boundaries ('le découpage electoral') on the grounds that this was something which only parliament should decide. He also, later in the same month, made good use of the student protests in the Latin quarter against a new law increasing university fees, and possibly introducing a measure of selection, to increase his popularity.

In December 1986, the education minister, Léon Devaquet, introduced a bill intended to reduce the overcrowding which had been one of the main factors in sparking off the 1968 revolt, and which still existed, by increasing the tuition fee for undergraduates and introducing a measure of selection. The widespread protests at what was seen as a fundamentally undemocratic measure were put down with their customary brutality by the French police, and a student of Algerian origin, Malik Ousekine, was killed.

Mitterrand had already let it be known that he was opposed to the *projet Devaquet*, and a cartoon by Plantu on the front page of *Le Monde* showed him grinning with satisfaction as he walked among the protestors in tattered jeans and with a ghetto blaster on his shoulder. On December 8, 1986, he paid a formal visit to Malik Ousekine's family to express his sympathy, and the final result of his very open opposition was that *le projet Devaquet* was withdrawn and the minister resigned. It was another example of the way in which he used his standing as president to undermine the popularity of the Chirac government and which helps to explain, when the next presidential election took place, why he beat Jacques Chirac by a more comfortable margin in the run-off on May 8 than he had obtained against Giscard d'Estaing on May 10, 1981.

There were nine candidates in the first ballot, on April 24, 1986, with the scores they obtained reflecting the divisions on both the right and left. Mitterrand came first, with Chirac second, and Raymond Barre, Giscard d'Estaing's prime minister between 1976 and 1981, third. In the run-off, Mitterrand beat Chirac by 16,704,279 votes against 14,218,970, a majority of 2,485,309 or 5.4 per cent of the votes cast. As in all previous presidential elections, except that of 1969, turn out was high, with 79.72 per cent of the electorate voting in the first round, and 81 per cent in the second. Chirac was understandably disappointed, though less so than Valéry Giscard d'Estaing had been in 1981. According to his *Mémoires*, he did not look at the political pages of a newspaper, or watch the television news until 1988, for fear of seeing his name mentioned.[6] Chirac was made of sterner stuff, and immediately began to try to work out why he had lost.

He did not, it would appear, entirely endorse the opinion of his wife, Bernadette, who is said to have commented that it was another sign that the French did not really like her husband, but acknowledged that he had used 'too technocratic' a language. His more vigorously right-wing ally Charles Pasqua attributed his defeat to the divisions on the right. In particular, he wondered whether it would be more appropriate to ask Le Pen how much longer he intended to continue putting the left in power. The general supposition in the Chirac camp was, perhaps understandably, that it was he who had lost rather than Mitterrand who had won, and that his defeat was due mainly to disunity. There were, however, other equally important factors.

In December 30, 1981, the Mauroy government had introduced one of its most popular measures, a wealth tax or *impôt sur les grandes fortunes*. It was inspired by the idea, not entirely peculiar to France but not used as a basis for fiscal policy elsewhere, that anyone very rich must have made at least some of their money by not declaring all their income to the tax authorities. It was also what the French call un *impôt de solidarité*, a Robin Hood-style tax justified by the idea that it is a good thing to take money from the rich and give it to the poor, and was understandably popular with everyone except those required to pay it. One of the first acts of the Chirac government, on April 6, 1986, was to abolish *l'impôt sur les grandes fortunes*, while at the same time reducing company taxation and taxes on dividends.

In 1982, the Mauroy government had also introduced what was called *l'autorisation administrative de licenciement*, the need for employers to obtain official permission before making anybody redundant. This had been seen as one of the principal means whereby the state could protect employees against employers anxious to maximise their profits by reducing their workforce, and had been understandably popular. Its abolition by the Chirac government on May 25, 1986 may have been, for the free-market economists (*les économistes libéraux*) who approved of what he was doing, a justifiable attempt to make the French labour force more flexible. Its disappearance nevertheless gave the impression that Chirac, for all his talk about national solidarity, was following the example of Margaret Thatcher and Ronald Reagan and encouraging the development of what is rather nicely known in French as *le capitalisme sauvage*. It is 'sauvage', in the sense that *le camping sauvage* is camping not governed by any rules, such as camping in a field and not in an officially approved camp site. But it is also savage, in the sense of brutal, to those who cannot keep up with its demands.

Mitterrand's unexpectedly large margin of victory in the 1988 presidential election was thus due, somewhat paradoxically, to the fact that he looked more of a conservative than the excessively energetic and radically-minded Jacques Chirac. Mitterrand, it was felt, could be relied upon to protect what the French call *les droits acquis*, the social advantages given to them by earlier governments. During the 1988 presidential election campaign, Laurent Fabius said that it was time to put an end to the 'game of ping-pong' between supporters of nationalisation and of privatisation. The idea was taken up by Mitterrand in one of the *petites phrases* which characterise French political discourse when he said that there would, in future, be 'ni privatisations, ni nationalisations'.

1988–95

If Mitterrand had kept the promise contained in number 45 of the *110 Propositions pour la France* to make the presidential mandate into a seven-year, non-renewable period of office, his reputation would probably stand much higher that it currently does. Since he was, by that time, almost 72, he could have told himself, with some justice, that he had had a good run for his money, and that his decision to leave office had given a younger man the opportunity of showing what he could do. It would also have made the various unflattering revelations of the mid-1990s much less interesting to the public.

As it was, however, Mitterrand chose to soldier on until 1995. He took no major initiatives either in home or foreign affairs, though he did break with tradition in one respect. When, on August 2, 1990, Saddam Hussein sent his troops into Kuwait, France sided with the United States, and French forces took part in the operation Desert Storm which drove Iraqi forces out of Kuwait in January–February 1991. It gave Mitterrand one of his highest ratings in the public opinion polls which are so marked a feature of French political life, with 62 per cent of those questioned in January 1991 approving his attitude, and there was little support for the action of the defence minister, Jean-Pierre Chevènement, when he resigned in protest on January 29.

The experience of *cohabitation* between 1986 and 1988 was made easier by the fact that little divided Mitterrand and Chirac on foreign policy. They represented France jointly at the Tokyo economic summit between May 4 and May 6, 1986, where Jacques Chirac seemed to have no objection to the reading of the Constitution which gives the principal responsibility for foreign affairs to the president. He was nevertheless there to remind the other six industrial nations of the statements in Articles 20 and 21 of the Constitution of the Fifth Republic: that the government 'determine et conduit la politique de la nation' (decides and carries out national policy), and that the prime minister 'dirige l'action du gouvernment' (directs the action of the government).

Once *la cohabitation* was in force, the suspicion that France might be absorbed into a Federal Europe, which Chirac had expressed with such vehemence in his *appel de Cochin* on December 6, 1978, took on a different appearance. It seemed to have been more the expression of his hostility towards Giscard d'Estaing than the statement of a permanent attitude. He and Mitterrand saw very much eye to eye on European matters as well as on foreign policy in general. When, on

April 12, 1986, the United States asked permission for its planes to fly over French territory in order to bomb Libya, the only disagreement between Chirac and Mitterrand was over which of them had taken the initiative in refusing.[7]

After his re-election on May 8, 1988, François Mitterrand once again used the power given to him by Article 12 of the 1958 Constitution to dissolve the Assemblée Nationale. On July 11, 1986, the Chirac government had re-established the *scrutin uninominal à deux tours*, and the legislative elections were held on June 5 and June 12. When the second round gave 277 seats to the Socialist Party and 27 to the Parti Communiste Français, the left had a theoretical overall majority of 32 against a right made up of 130 UDF, 128 RPR and 4 députés representing various other right-wing parties.

This time, it included only one for the Front National, an example of the advantages of the single member two ballot system over proportional representation. When a party represents so unpleasant a point of view as the National Front, it is difficult, if not always impossible, for it to form the electoral alliances essential if it is to win seats on the second ballot. If no candidates, either on the right or on the left, are prepared to stand down in its favour on the second ballot, there is no chance of its winning more than the occasional seat.

Since the Communist Party had made it clear that it would not automatically support a socialist government, the confirmation on June 14 of Michel Rocard in the post of prime minister to which Mitterrand had appointed him on May 10, placed him at the head of what was in fact a minority administration: 277 for the Parti Socialiste; 289 for all the other parties in the unlikely event of their wishing to combine. On May 15, 1991, Mitterrand took a minor but historic step in French politics by appointing Édith Cresson as prime minister. He did so, it was rumoured, partly to prevent Michel Rocard, whom she replaced, from becoming popular enough to be the socialist candidate in the 1995 presidential election. She held office for only eleven months, a shorter time than any other prime minister of the Fifth Republic, and is remembered abroad mainly for her lack of tact in talking about other countries, describing the Japanese as having all the characteristics of ants, and opining that all Englishmen must be homosexuals because none of the men in London turned round to look at her as she walked along the street.

In France itself, where such opinions were perhaps more widely held than the criticism of her in enlightened circles suggested, she earned herself the undying hostility of the civil service establishment by deciding, on November 7, 1991, that L'École Nationale d'Administration should be moved to Strasbourg. She annoyed her more liberally-minded colleagues by suggesting, on July 9, 1994, that there were so many unwanted immigrants, especially of non-Caucasian origin, that the government would have to charter jumbo jets to send back home anyone who was in France illegally (*les sans papiers*).

Although the transfer of L'École Nationale d'Administration to Strasbourg was justifiable on empirical and political grounds, it was more widely attributed, within the civil service itself, to personal considerations. It was all very well for by Édith Cresson to talk about the need to move as many government offices as possible out of Paris. It was also superficially convincing for her to argue that to have the École Nationale d'Administration nearer to Germany was a sign of France's attachment to the cause of European integration. The fact remained that she was herself a product of one of the privately-run Grandes Écoles, L'École des Hautes Études Commerciales (HEC), which was to remain in the Paris area. In the event, only part of the teaching offered by l'ÉNA was moved to Strasbourg, and the 1997 *Rapport public de la Cour des Comptes*, compiled by civil servants who were almost all former pupils of the École Nationale d'Administration, took particular pleasure in underlining how wasteful of the tax-payer's money the whole operation had been.[8]

On April 2, 1992, Madame Cresson was replaced by Pierre Bérégovoy, and followed what was rapidly becoming the tradition whereby politicians who have been unsuccessful on a national level are appointed to high office in Brussels. She became one of France's two members of the European Commission. Bérégovoy was the only prime minister in France ever to have begun life as a member of the industrial working class. He trained as a gas fitter, and had completed his education by taking courses in management before becoming, from 1958 onwards, a professional politician. In 1969, he became a member of the central committee of the Socialist Party, and in 1983 mayor for the town of Nevers, a post he combined from 1988 onward with that of député. Between 1984 and 1986, and again between 1988 and 1992, he was Ministre de l'Économie et des Finances, a post in which his highly orthodox, monetarist policies of competitive deflation did little for either Michel Rocard's or Édith Cresson's popularity.

On May 1, 1993, however, Pierre Bérégovoy committed suicide, using the revolver which he had, inexplicably, managed to take away from his chauffeur and bodyguard without the latter noticing. He had, understandably, been depressed by the size of the defeat which the Socialist Party had sustained in the legislative elections held in the previous March. Together with its allies, it had won only 67 seats, as against a right-wing majority of 428, made up of 208 seats for the Union pour la Démocratie Française and 242 for Jacques Chirac's Rassemblement pour la République.

This had required Mitterrand to undergo his second experience of *cohabitation*, this time with the urbane Édouard Balladur, of whom more later, instead of the less amenable Jacques Chirac, who had declined to serve in the same post again. But it was less the political defeat of the Socialist Party which led to Bérégovoy's suicide than the revelation by *Le Canard enchaîné*, on February 3, 1993 that he had received an interest free loan of 1,000,000 francs (£100,000 or $US150,000) to buy his Paris apartment. The fact had come to light in the course of the investigation which the *juge d'instruction* (examining magistrate), Thierry Jean-Pierre, had been carrying out into the affairs of a businessman, Roger-Patrice Pelat, who had already been implicated, in February 1989, in rather suspect take-over by Péchiney of the American-owned firm of American Can.

There had, at the time, been some talk of insider dealing (*délit d'initié*), with the possibility that since Péchiney was partly state-owned, information about the impending take over had been leaked from official sources. What was particularly embarrassing was that Pelat was one of Mitterrand's oldest friends. The two had met and become friends in a German prisoner of war camp in 1940, and on February 16, 1989, Mitterrand gave a long interview in which he argued that there was no reason, simply because Pelat had started life very poor, and ended up very rich, why he should put an end to their friendship. Although there was never any suggestion that Mitterrand himself had ever been involved, at any period in his life, in any financial dealings which were in any way open to criticism, the impression grew that he was not very good at choosing his friends. He had also, it was revealed in 1991, remained friendly with René Bousquet, the former general secretary of the police force under Vichy, who was assassinated on June 8, 1993 before he could be brought to trial.

On November 11, 1992, when he went to lay a wreath on the tomb of Marshal Pétain, Mitterrand gave further evidence of his view that the French should learn to forgive and forget the less honourable aspects of their behaviour during the second world war. He did not, unlike de Gaulle, pretend that the Vichy régime represented only a small majority of the French people, and on September 11, 1994, shortly after the publication of Patrice Péan's book, *Une Jeunesse française*, made a plea for national reconciliation. Its only weakness lay in his claim that he knew nothing of the anti-semitic laws introduced by the Vichy régime as early as October 1940. He had, it is true, been in a prisoner of war camp until December 1941, but it was scarcely conceivable, as was widely pointed out, that a man as closely involved as he was with the Vichy régime from January 1942 until early in 1943 knew nothing of the nature of these laws or of the date when they had been introduced.

Taken by themselves, these revelations about Mitterrand's early life might not have done his standing all that much harm. His behaviour had, after all, been typical of a large number of French civil servants and politicians. Not a single French judge, it was pointed out, resigned in protest against the actions of the Vichy government. But coming on top of the suicide not only of Pierre Bérégovoy but also of another of Mitterrand's close associates, François de Grossouvre, who killed himself in his office at the Élysée Palace on April 7, 1994, they strengthened the impression that the Mitterrand years, which had begun with such optimism in May 1981, were ending in an atmosphere of total disillusionment.

Matters were not improved by a number of other affairs which reflected poorly either on the honesty or the competence of the people whom Mitterrand had called upon to govern. The most serious of these was the realisation, in the mid-1980s, that some 10,000 haemophiliacs had been infected with the AIDS virus ('Le Sida') as a result of having been supplied with blood collected from prison inmates. The high incidence of drug taking and homosexuality in prisons made infections of this type an obvious danger, but one which, it was later argued, could have been avoided if the French medical authorities had agreed to use the Abbott test, developed in America, and aimed at checking that blood was free from contamination.

It was, however, alleged that the French postponed the use and commercialisation of the Abbott test until a comparable test had been developed by French scientists, and that the root cause of the 'scandale du sang contaminé' was French anti-Americanism. This may or may not be true, and the matter was vigorously debated. Anti-Americanism is a cross-party phenomenon in France, so that it is improbable that a right-wing government would have acted differently from the socialist administration which was in charge in 1984–5 when the infected blood was distributed.

The fact, however, that the minister of health at the time, Georgina Dufoix, said that she felt 'responsable mais non coupable' (responsible but not guilty), and that no charge of negligence was then brought against Laurent Fabius, the then prime minister, strengthened the impression that the Socialist Party had become highly skilled at not paying any price for its mistakes. When the director of the blood transfusion service, Dr Michel Garetta, was sentenced in October 1982 to four years in prison, the comment most frequently heard was 'c'est lui le lampiste' (he's being made to carry the can). He did not make any money out of the distribution of contaminated blood.

For the general public, especially for anyone with an interest in football, it is perhaps the career of the businessman Bernard Tapie which best illustrates the climate dominating the closing years of Mitterrand's second presidency. In the 1980s, especially after the socialists had begun to discover the virtues of capitalist enterprise, Tapie had been celebrated as the incarnation of 'la France qui gagne' (the France that wins). He even, it is alleged, bought the firm of Adidas with money lent to him on Mitterrand's instructions by one of the French nationalised banks.[9] He took over companies in difficulty, made them prosperous, created jobs, and made such an impression both on Mitterrand and on Michel Rocard that on April 4, 1992, he was made Ministre de la Ville. However, on May 23, he was forced to resign, and on December 12, 1993, the Assemblée Nationale voted to deprive him of his parliamentary immunity so that he could face charges of misuse of public money, fraud, and tax evasion. He was declared bankrupt, accused of match fixing, and is currently busy trying to avoid a jail sentence.

Events of this kind, accompanied by the fact that another politician who held ministerial office under Mitterrand, Alain Carignon, had actually been sent to prison for five years on charges of corruption, naturally tend to overshadow the achievements of the fourteen years in which he held office. Had these achievements included the reduction of unemployment, instead of a rise in the jobless from 1.5 million to over 3 million, both Mitterrand's own behaviour and that of some of his ministers would not have incurred so harsh a verdict. He would have done what he had been elected to do, and would also have been less criticised as a man as well as a politician if the policies followed during his years had brought about a reduction in social inequalities in France. As it was, however, a study by the Institut des Études Sociales et Economics (INSEE) in 1991 showed that the gap between rich and poor had widened in the France of François Mitterrand just as much as it had in the Great Britain of Margaret Thatcher.

It was Mitterrand's great misfortune to have come to power at the wrong time. Had he won the presidential election in 1965, or even in 1974, the story might have been very different, and the similarity between his successes and those which Giscard d'Estaing might have enjoyed if he had won the presidential election of 1974 would have been less marked. He too would have carried on with the policy of trying to unify Europe within the framework of what, on November 1, 1993, officially became the European Union. He might even have won the referendum of September 20, 1992 ratifying the Maastricht Treaty by a slightly larger margin than the 51.05 per cent against 59.95 per cent that Mitterrand obtained. Since he also suggested in 1995 that the franc might benefit from a further devaluation in relation to the German mark, he might even have been more successful in reducing unemployment.

What is even more certain is that Giscard d'Estaing, like Mitterrand, would have made the Constitution of the Fifth Republic work in order to provide what is, when seen in an international context, an extraordinarily stable and tolerant society. France under the Mitterrand presidency, like Great Britain under Margaret Thatcher or the United States in the years of Ronald Reagan, remained a country in which the rule of law was far more widely observed than it was broken, in which the state did not persecute its citizens but did its best to carry out its duty of protecting them, in which the press was free and the courts offered recourse to all citizens against the arbitrary actions of the executive power. It is more than can be said either of states with a predominantly Islamic culture, or indeed of any country which has remained untouched by the triple blessings of the Protestant revolution of the sixteenth century, the ideals of the eighteenth-century Enlightenment, or the achievements of the industrial revolution.

5   Jacques Chirac
The impulsive grandson

Generalities

Jacques Chirac is the first president of the Fifth Republic to have made a major political miscalculation: his announcement, on April 21, 1997, that he was dissolving the National Assembly which he had inherited on being elected president on May 7, 1995, and in which his own party, the Rassemblement pour la République (RPR), had 258 seats, and its ally, the Union pour la Démocratie Française (UDF) 206, as against a bare 56 for the Socialist Party. For when the results of the second round of the elections were announced on June 1, the situation had changed quite dramatically. The left had 319 seats, and the right 245. Chirac thus found himself in the unprecedented position of a president who still had over six years of office before him, but had deprived himself of the parliamentary majority he needed to carry out his policies.

This may turn out to have less serious consequences than first thought. If anything, it could well have the paradoxical effect of strengthening the institutions of the Fifth Republic by showing how they can be made to adapt to yet another development which their founder had not anticipated, that of a long period of *cohabitation* between left and right. It has already, as I shall explain later, provided a reminder of how thoroughly bi-partisan a number of French national policies have become, especially in the area of foreign affairs and in France's relationship with the European Union. But it was not, at least in the first instance, an auspicious beginning to the realisation of what had always been Chirac's fondest dream, that of being elected president of the Republic. The photographs of him in the newspapers in the months following the publication of the results of June 1 looked like those of a man who did not quite understand what had happened to him, but knew that he did not like it.

Other presidents, especially in the eyes of the outside world, had acted with a certain lack of wisdom, as well as with a marked absence of consideration for the countries with which France was theoretically in alliance. When General de Gaulle used his speech in Montréal on July 26 1967 to offer open encouragement to the Quebec separatist movement, he was insulting one of France's oldest allies in NATO. François Mitterrand's appearance on French television on August 19, 1991, brandishing a letter of reassurance from the communist hard-liners who had just launched the Moscow putsch which tried to overthrow Gorbachev, was an act which he himself soon came to regret. Similarly, Giscard d'Estaing never recovered his reputation as an international statesman which he lost by going to visit Brezhnev in Warsaw on May 19, 1980, a bare five months after the Soviet invasion of Afghanistan. Only Jacques Chirac, however, has so far made a mistake whose immediate effect seemed to be to weaken the president's position within France itself.

The fact that he did so after achieving what had clearly been a life-time ambition to become president, and which he had fulfilled, as Mitterrand had done, only on his third attempt, made the situation in which he had placed himself particularly ironic. He had always presented himself as one of the most faithful followers of Charles de Gaulle, and this was a tradition based on the idea of a strong president able to carry out his policies with the help of a comfortable parliamentary majority. The name of the party which he had founded on December 5, 1976, the Rassemblement pour la République (RPR), had been deliberately chosen to evoke de Gaulle's Rassemblement du Peuple Français (RPF), and he had chosen a particularly symbolic date and place to announce his candidacy for the presidential election of April 25 and May 7, 1995. He had done so on November 4, 1994, thirty years to the day after de Gaulle had announced his own candidacy in 1965, on the feast day of Saint Charles, and in Lille, de Gaulle's own birthplace. His intention throughout the presidential election campaign of 1995 had been to present himself as the true heir of the Gaullist tradition. Why, then, did he make the mistake that he did?

The official reason which Chirac himself gave for his decision to dissolve the National Assembly was that he needed what he called *un nouvel élan* in order to carry out the reforms made necessary by what he described, in his televised address to the nation on April 21, 'le long laisser aller dont nous payons toujours le prix'. It was his way of refer-ring to the fourteen years in which François Mitterrand had been president, and during which the right had not really been able, even during the two periods of *cohabitation* between 1986 and 1988, and between 1993 and 1995, to put all its policies fully into effect. He may also have been misled not only by the public opinion polls, all of which promised a victory for the right in the legislative elections of May–June 1997, but also by the fact that when other presidents had used the power given to them by Article 12 of the 1958 Constitution to dissolve the National Assembly, they had won important electoral victories by so doing.

De Gaulle had done so twice: on October 10, 1962, in the middle of the 1962 referendum campaign for the election of the president of the Republic by universal suffrage; and then on May 30, 1968, after it had become clear that the attempt by the student radicals to overthrow the Fifth Republic had failed. On both occasions he had considerably increased the number of seats of the political groupings prepared to support him. François Mitterrand had shown himself equally adept in the skill most necessary to being a successful British prime minister, that of the timing of the next general election. On May 22, 1981, after having been elected president on May 10, he dissolved the National Assembly, and the Socialist Party won an absolute majority of 269 seats out of the 491. After being re-elected for a second term on May 8, 1988, he dissolved the National Assembly, which since the election of March 1986 had had a right-wing majority of 276 seats against 215 for the left. He won a majority of 61 seats, enough to keep the left-wing alliance known as *la majorité présidentielle* comfortably in power until 1993.

Chirac would also have been aware of another pattern in French legislative elections since 1958: whenever a president waits for legislative elections held at the normal time, he tends to lose. This happened most dramatically in March 1993, when the *majorité présidentielle* of 282 went down to 56 for the Socialist Party and 28 for its non-communist allies. In 1967, under the presidency of Georges Pompidou, the Gaullist Union pour la Nouvelle République (UNR) saw its majority reduced to one single seat, and François Mitterrand's Socialist Party lost the elections of March 1986.

Chirac also knew that there would, in any case, have to be parliamentary elections in the spring or early summer of 1998. Rather than run the risk of losing them, he decided to trust the public opinion polls and hold what are called 'des élections législatives anticipées'. His decision to do so may also have been influenced by the unpopularity of his prime minister, Alain Juppé, and by the absence in the ranks of leading Gaullists of anyone else prepared to support the adoption by France of the Euro in 1999. Neither Philippe Séguin nor Charles

Pasqua was keen on the idea, and Chirac had staked his reputation on making France ready to be in the first wave of the single European currency.

If Chirac had dissolved the National Assembly in 1995, immediately on being elected, he might have got away with it. Unfortunately for him, he waited ten months, giving the Socialist Party the opportunity of continuing its recovery from its calamitous defeat in the legislative elections of March 1993. This recovery had already begun with the unexpectedly good showing of its candidate, Lionel Jospin, in the presidential elections of April 23 and May 7, 1995, and the legislative elections of May 25 and June 1, 1997, were to confirm that this was no flash in the pan.

The Socialist Party and its immediate allies won 246 seats, as against the 56 it had had since March 1993. The Communist Party increased its score from 24 to 37, the other left-wing parties went up to 26, and the ecologists won 8 seats. The Rassemblement pour la République, in contrast, had only 139, and the party originally founded by Giscard d'Estaing, the Union pour la Démocratie Française, 109. Other right-wing parties won 7, and the Front National only one. What became known as *la gauche plurielle*, the alliance between socialists, radicals, communists and ecologists, thus had a parliamentary majority of 66.

These results gave Chirac no choice but to appoint the first secretary of the Socialist Party, Lionel Jospin, as prime minister, and to ask him to form a government. As in March 1986, when François Mitterrand's Socialist Party had lost the legislative elections, and again when the same thing had happened in March 1993, *la cohabitation* was inevitable. This time, however, there were three important differences, of which the first, and most obvious, was that it was now a right-wing president who found himself obliged to appoint a left-wing prime minister. The second was that Chirac, who had been prime minister in the first *cohabitation*, under François Mitterrand, was now president himself.

The third was that with the next presidential election not being due until 2002, the arrangement looked as if it might last for five years, instead of the two during which Mitterrand had worked with Chirac between 1986 and 1988, and then with Édouard Balladur between 1993 and 1995. The institutions of the Fifth Republic were working smoothly enough, and *l'alternance* had become a sufficiently familiar feature of the French political landscape for the word to be far less frequently used than it had been when the left first took power in 1981.

But they were not working as either de Gaulle, or, perhaps more importantly in his own eyes, Jacques Chirac, thought that they should.

The Socialist Party of Lionel Jospin was not, it is true, inspired by the same passion for Keynesian pump-priming or Attlee-style nationalisation as the same party had been under François Mitterrand in 1981. Far from seeking to extend public ownership, it proceeded to allow the partial privatisation of France-Télécom, the sale of 49 per cent of the state's holding in Air-France, and the sale of the state-owned insurance company, the Groupe des Assurances Nationales, (le GAN). The term used may be different, in that the operations began to be known technically as *des transferts*. But the final result was the same, in that decisions previously made by the state came more and more to be replaced, in France as in other advanced industrial countries, by individual choices made by the managers of private companies.

But while this is very much the same policy which Chirac himself had encouraged when he was prime minister under François Mitterrand, the same is not true of the major device adopted by the left for reducing unemployment, the reduction of the working week from 39 to 35 hours by 2001, with no loss of pay. In spite of Chirac's very clearly stated disapproval for such a measure, the Jospin government obtained parliamentary approval for it in February 1998, and the presidency gives Chirac no power of veto to prevent it from being implemented. The Fifth Republic, conceived by de Gaulle as a régime in which the president takes the major decisions on policy, leaving it to parliament to pass the necessary legislation and the prime minister to implement it, had turned into something very different. It had become, to all appearances, a régime in which the president retained some useful formal powers, but where the last word remained with parliament, with the president's position being in some respects more like that of a constitutional monarch.

The president of the Fifth Republic continues to retain an important advantage over a constitutional monarch. He has acceded to his position by election, not by inheritance. This gives him the right, which a monarch does not have, to play a political role. But when he lacks a parliamentary party to support him, the power which he has to play this role is essentially a moral one. It also depends very much on his ability to act behind the scenes, and he has to be very careful about the use which he makes of one particular right which the Constitution gives him. For while he may, in accordance with Article 12 of the Constitution, dissolve the National Assembly after one year, this is a weapon which he has to use very carefully, and which can easily backfire in his hand. For if Jacques Chirac were to dissolve parliament again, and be disappointed a second time in his hope that the elections which he had just brought about would give him the kind of majority he wanted, he would be like a suitor who had twice seen his marriage proposal declined.

This explains why political commentators, especially of the right, began to talk about this *cohabitation* as looking as though it might become a permanent feature of the political scene. They generally did so with disapproval, speaking in tones of shocked horror of either a return to the Fourth Republic or even of the beginning of a Sixth. The comparison with the Fourth Republic was obvious, in that power had quite visibly shifted from the president to the prime minister. This had always implicitly been the case, since even de Gaulle and Pompidou would not have been able to govern as they did if they had had to face a hostile majority in the Assemblée Nationale. But between 1986 and 1988, as between 1993 and 1995, the similarity between the Fourth and Fifth Republics had been overshadowed both by Mitterrand's own skill as a politician and by the relatively short period separating the parliamentary election from the next presidential election.

Now, however, France looked as if it might be moving towards a version of democracy which had more in common with what happens in the United States than with the Constitution which de Gaulle had in mind when he came back to power in 1958. In what had indeed begun to look, to any observer of how the Constitution worked in practice, rather like a Sixth French Republic, the election of a new president, or the re-election of the current holder of the office, was going to coincide with the election of a new legislative chamber. Both the president and the députés of the current Assemblée Nationale are, at the moment of writing[1] due to stand for re-election in the spring or early summer of 2002.

It would be surprising if such a coincidence recurred on a regular basis in France, at least in the foreseeable future. Unlike Georges Pompidou, Jacques Chirac has never given any sign of wishing to reduce the presidential mandate to five years. The French are probably too attached to the idea of full parliamentary elections held on a five-year basis to adopt the American system whereby half the seats in the House of Representatives, and a third of those in the Senate, are renewed on the same day that the presidential election takes place. But unless Chirac dissolves the Assembly for a second time, in the hope that he will then obtain *une majorité présidentielle* to replace that of *la gauche plurielle* currently supporting the socialist administration of

Lionel Jospin, the elections of 2002 will have a touch of the American system about them.

This will, naturally, only be the case if he decides to soldier on with Lionel Jospin. Predictions as to whether he chooses to do so may turn out to have merely an historical value of their own, and to turn out to be as inaccurate as the predictions of the French High Command in the 1930s as to how the German army was going to behave in any future war. There are nevertheless several reasons why Chirac might chose to cohabit for five years, of which the first and most important is the bi-partisan nature of French policy both towards Europe and in foreign affairs in general.

Ever since de Gaulle's historic meetings with Konrad Adenauer in the late 1950s and early 1960s, culminating in the signature on January 14, 1963 of the agreement on Franco–German co-operation, French policy has been increasingly dominated by a closer relationship with Germany within the framework of the European Union. Although both Georges Pompidou and Valéry Giscard d'Estaing moderated the hostility towards the United Kingdom and the United States which de Gaulle seemed to see as a natural corollary to France's closer ties with Germany, they did not basically change the fundamental direction of France's European policy.

The crucial decision by François Mitterrand, in March 1983, to keep the franc within the European Exchange Rate Mechanism confirmed the central importance of this relationship in an economic context. The fact that it should have been a socialist who took the decision to keep the close link between the franc and the mark underlined the strongly bi-partisan flavour to France's European policy. It was also Mitterrand who urged the acceptance by France of the Maastricht treaty of February 1992, and of the convergence criteria for the introduction of the Euro on January 1, 1999. Since this is not a policy which either Lionel Jospin or the current Socialist Party have ever called into question, the only real difference between left and right in current economic policy concerns the reduction of the working week to thirty-five hours with no loss of pay.

On other issues, the *cohabitation* between Jospin and Chirac looks quite likely to last, with the welcome if paradoxical effect of making Jacques Chirac's mistake in calling the parliamentary elections when he did so seem far less serious than when the results were first announced. Both he and Jospin are in favour of the strict monetary discipline required of a country wishing to replace its national currency by the Euro: an annual budget deficit of 3 per cent or less of the Gross National Product; a public sector debt of less than 60 per cent of its GNP; and an inflation rate no higher than the average of the three countries in the European Union with the lowest annual rate.

Since both major political groupings in France support the banker's agenda implicit in the Maastricht convergence criteria, there is thus little danger of a serious conflict on economic policy between Jacques Chirac and Lionel Jospin. While this is fortunate for those who believe, as de Gaulle himself did, that France's future lies in a united Europe, it is another factor which makes Chirac's decision to hold legislative elections in the early summer of 1997 seem less of a long-term blunder than it looked at the time. One of the reasons given for this decision was that he needed a more solid and united majority than the one which he had inherited if he was to see France successfully through to the introduction of the Euro on January 1, 1999. Since there is virtually complete agreement among all the main political parties on what needs to be done to enable this to happen, Chirac might just as well have saved himself the humiliation.

Chirac also enjoys a good relationship with Jospin's foreign minister, Hubert Védrine (1944–). He too is a former pupil of the École Nationale d'Administration, and shares the Gaullist view that the United States is too powerful a country for its dominance not to need challenging by the only country which he sees capable of doing this, which is France. During the crisis of February 1998 about weapons inspections in Iraq, Védrine worked in total harmony with Chirac in playing what both men saw as a decisive role in persuading Saddam Hussein to accept the mediation offer of the United Nations Secretary General, Kofi Annan. France even lent Kofi Annan a French aeroplane in which to fly from Paris to Baghdad, pointing out to him that to arrive in an American aircraft would not strengthen his chances of persuading Saddam Hussein to agree to the free inspection of suspected weapon-making sites.

The only real problems are those which may arise if Chirac reproduces some of the curious behaviour which has, from time to time, punctuated his long political career.

1932–95

His political career began in 1967, when he was 35, and had already had a distinguished and successful career in the army and civil service. His father, François Chirac, was the son of a primary schoolmaster (*instituteur*), Louis Chirac, who had become headteacher at a school in Brive-la-Gaillarde, one of the principal towns in the Département de la Corrèze, not far from Georges Pompidou's home village of Montboudif, in Le Cantal.

Initially, François Chirac worked in a bank, which he left in 1936 to work as a manager for the aeroplane manufacturing company of Porez. This involved a move to Paris, where his only son, Jacques, was born on November 29, 1932. François Chirac's first-born child, a daughter, was born in 1926, but died at the age of two. Jacques Chirac was thus, to all intents and purposes, an only child, and one to whom the remark made by Bernard Shaw seems particularly appropriate: 'Never worry about an only son. The thought of failure will never cross his mind'. Since de Gaulle was born in Lille, Pompidou in Montboudif, Valéry Giscard d'Estaing in Koblenz and François Mitterrand in Jarnac, Chirac is thus so far the only president of the Fifth Republic to have been born in Paris.

Until 1950, Jacques Chirac received the traditional education of a child of the French professional middle class: studies at the local primary school, followed by courses at the lycée Hoche, at Saint-Cloud, and at the lycées Carnot and Louis-le-Grand. At the age of 18, however, he gave the first visible signs of his independence of spirit when he embarked as an apprentice on a cargo boat bound for America. After three months he gave way to his father's plea that he should follow a more normal career. In September 1951, he went to the École libre des Sciences Politiques, and in 1954 was successful in the *concours d'entrée* at the École Nationale d'Administration.

Before taking up his place, he had to do his military service, and was not at all unhappy at the prospect. He entered the cavalry school at Saumur, and although he did well enough to come out top (*major*) in the *concours de sortie*, was initially refused the distinction for political reasons. In 1950, he had signed the Stockholm appeal, launched on March 3 of that year by the communist-inspired Peace Movement, which sought to impose a ban on all atomic weapons. This made him suspect to the French establishment, and especially to the military authorities, and it needed the intervention of General Koenig, head of the French General Staff, for him to be given the top ranking he deserved. A similar incident, it will be recalled, took place in 1924, when only Pétain's intervention on behalf of de Gaulle led the examiners at the École de Guerre to give him to final mark of *bien* instead of their intended *passable*.

It was also General Koenig's intervention which enabled Chirac to achieve what was an unusual ambition among French students in the 1950s, that of being sent to join the army on active service in Algeria. Between April 1956 and June 1957, he served with distinction as a lieutenant in the élite regiment of the Chasseurs d'Afrique, and later described the fifteen months he spent fighting in Algeria as the happiest period of his life.[2] Indeed, in spite of having been wounded in the face in one of the clashes between his platoon and the FLN, he tried to stay in Algeria after his normal turn of duty was over, but was told that it was now time for him to learn to serve the state in another capacity, that of a career civil servant.

On March 16, 1956, while still in the army, he had married Bernadette de Courcel, the daughter of a family which was not only well established in the French aristocracy but also had impeccable Gaullist credentials. The founder of the family, Louis Chodron, had been an assistant to Napoleon I's foreign minister Talleyrand (1754–1838), and in 1852 had been granted the right by Napoleon III to call himself de Courcel. Although his wife thus belonged only to the Imperial nobility, Chirac nevertheless married into a family with a longer tradition in the aristocracy than that of Giscard d'Estaing, and the fact that her uncle, Geoffrey de Courcel, had been aide-de-camp to de Gaulle did nothing to harm his future political career.

Bernadette's mother, who belonged an older aristocratic family, that of de Brondeau, would apparently have preferred someone from a better background than this 'petit-fils d'instituteur radical qui ne fréquente pas l'Église'.[3] She cannot, however, have been entirely disappointed at the outcome, especially since Chirac later became quite assiduous in his attendance at Mass. The couple had two daughters, Laurence and Claude. The former, though a brilliant student in her early youth, fell ill with anorexia. Claude, her younger sister, has identified herself much more strongly than her mother has with her father's political career, and apparently differs from him only in not wishing to reduce the number of English and American pop songs played on the French radio. She has become one of his closest public relations advisers, paying particular attention to the image which he projects through his choice of clothes, and especially ties. Bernadette, in addition to concerning herself with good works, a well-established tradition for the wife of a president of the French Republic, has also followed a political career of her own as conseillère générale de Corrèze.

In 1957, Chirac took up his place at l'ÉNA, and in 1959 he came tenth in the *concours de sortie*. This enabled him to choose one of the Grands Corps, and he became a member of the Cour des Comptes. He was, however, already tempted by a political career, and in 1965, after a fairly rapid promotion to the rank of conseiller référendaire[4] was elected conseiller municipal in the *commune* of Ste Féréole, near Brive, in La Corrèze. In 1966, he stood unsuccessfully as a candidate in a by-election, again in the same area, before beginning his political career proper in the legislative elections of June 1967. In spite of the offer of a safe seat in the Paris area as a candidate of the Gaullist UDR (Union pour la Nouvelle République), he chose to stand in the traditionally very solidly left-wing Département de la Corrèze, winning the seat of Ussel which he held until his election as president of the Republic in May 1995.

Had he lost, a possibility which does not seem to have occurred to him in the course of a campaign in which he finally defeated his communist rival by a mere 537 votes, there was a safety net all ready. Georges Pompidou, who was prime minister at the time, would have been very happy to appoint him Directeur de l'aviation civile.[5] Chirac had already, before beginning his career as an elected politician, been closely associated with Pompidou, serving in his cabinet, or private office, in 1963, and being one of his most loyal friends.

Chirac is, however, apparently never happier than when electioneering, and even has a certain contempt for those who exercise political power in France without constantly requiring themselves to face the electorate. In 1994, when the general feeling was that if Jacques Delors, then still president of the European Commission, were to stand for election as the socialist candidate for the French presidency, he would certainly win, Chirac was one of the few right-wing politicians not to be worried. 'Calme-toi' he told his fellow Gaullist, Charles Pasqua, 'Delors ne se présentera pas. Comme Rocard, il fait partie des gens qui ont besoin d'être nommés' (Calm down. Delors won't stand. Like Rocard, he is one of those who needs to be appointed).[6]

This is another factor which makes his decision to hold the parliamentary elections of 1997 a year earlier than he needed to do so a surprising mistake. He, of all people, knows what elections are like, especially in the country areas which still return over half the members of the Assemblée Nationale. When his future prime minister and fellow *énarque*, Alain Juppé, was moving from the civil service into politics, he apparently said to him: 'Alors, vous voulez faire de la politique? J'espère que vous savez tâter le cul des vaches' (So, you want to go in for politics? I hope you're good at feeling cows' arses).[7]

One of the traditional functions which the French député is expected to fulfil is that of obtaining money from the central government to improve the facilities in his constituency. You can tell how good Chirac is at this the moment you cross into La Corrèze from one of the adjoining départements. There is a dramatic improvement in the quality of the road surface, a fact which is also a tribute to the influence he was able to exercise between 1970 and 1979 as Président du

Conseil Général de la Corrèze. He is, above all else, a professional politician, a more cultivated version of Lyndon B. Johnson, as irresistible a political force, though perhaps more on the local than the national level, as Margaret Thatcher was in her time. Georges Pompidou habitually referred to him as his 'bulldozer', and is reputed to have said that if he asked him to dig a tunnel from the Élysée Palace to the Palais Bourbon, the meeting place of the Assemblée Nationale, he would expect to wake up the next morning to see the work already well advanced.

Immediately after being elected député, Chirac became the youngest minister in Pompidou's fourth government, formed on April 6, 1967 after the narrow victory of the UNR at the elections of March 5 and March 12, when he was appointed Secrétaire d'État (junior minister) for employment. He gave solid support to Georges Pompidou during the events of May 1968, and served in a succession of more senior posts under Jacques Chaban-Delmas and Pierre Messmer. In particular, Messmer appointed him on July 5, 1972 as minister of agriculture in the government he formed after the resignation of Jacques Chaban-Delmas. It was one of the offices of state which Chirac most enjoyed, and he is a man who is most at home in what is known as *la France profonde*, the France of small country towns and of the small farmers who have managed to survive the impact of the European Common Agricultural Policy.

Chirac was deeply affected by the death of Georges Pompidou, whom he had seen as a kind of father figure in politics. Both, like François Mitterrand, were *des hommes du terroir*, men with solid roots in rural France, quite different in personality both from the aristocratic Giscard d'Estaing and Chirac's main rival for the presidency in 1995, Édouard Balladur. 'L'un est de la Nièvre', wrote Nicholas Domenach in 1997, when comparing Mitterrand with Chirac, 'l'autre de Corrèze. Balladur est de nulle part', and it is instructive to find so clear an echo in a book of the now virtually forgotten nationalist writer, Maurice Barrès (1862–1923), and his insistence on the need for real Frenchmen to prove their Frenchness by the depth of their provincial roots.

In this respect, it was as much a matter of personal temperament as political differences which led to the first incident in Chirac's career in which he gave signs of having other qualities associated with a bulldozer apart from irresistible efficiency. He is six years younger than Giscard d'Estaing, being only 42 as opposed to Giscard's 48 when Georges Pompidou's death in April 1974 created the need for another presidential election. Initially, he decided to support the candidacy of Pierre Messmer, but when Messmer withdrew in favour of the more dynamic traditional Gaullist, Jacques Chaban-Delmas, Chirac switched his allegiance to Giscard d'Estaing, bringing forty-two Gaullist députés with him.

It was a crucial move, since Giscard d'Estaing had never been popular with the traditional Gaullists. Even before the parliamentary elections of March 1967 had left the Gaullists dependent on the support of Giscard d'Estaing's forty-three Républicains Indépendants, he had annoyed them on January 10 1967 by his famous 'Oui, mais', and after de Gaulle's speech in Montreal, on July 23, 1967, had criticised what he called 'l'exercice solitaire du pouvoir'. He had then recommended a 'no' vote in the April 1969 referendum on regionalisation and the reform of the Senate. Chirac's support for Giscard d'Estaing was one of the main factors in the relatively low vote for Chaban-Delmas in the first round of the 1974 presidential elections, when he obtained only 12.24 per cent of the votes cast on May 5, as against 34.48 per cent for Mitterrand and 27.71 per cent for Giscard d'Estaing. Chirac again helped Giscard d'Estaing in his narrow victory, by a margin of not more than 1.15 per cent, in the second round against Mitterrand on May 19.

His appointment as prime minister was therefore something of a reward for services rendered. However, for reasons suggested in more detail in Chapter 3, the two men did not get on well together, largely because Chirac moved away from a Gaullist reading of the Constitution by insisting that the prime minister should be more than the person who simply finds means of implementing the policies which the president has chosen and wishes to see adopted. In so far as there was a difference on actual policy, it concerned the introduction of a capital gains tax (*la taxation des plus-values*), which Giscard d'Estaing favoured and Chirac did not. Chirac, as a more thorough-going Gaullist than Giscard d'Estaing, was also unhappy about what he saw as the softening of the hostility towards the United States.

But it was a clash of personalities rather than of policies, and of the different image which each man wanted to project of himself. Giscard d'Estaing was the technocrat who wanted to take France more in the direction of the consensual politics which he saw as characteristic of the English-speaking world, of a liberal society in which the state would play a less obvious and more relaxed role in influencing the lifestyle of its citizens than has traditionally been the case in France. Chirac, in contrast, has always been more of populist, and with more of de Gaulle's idea of the state playing a central role in national life.

These are, in a sense, what were to become the two faces of French conservatism. Although Chirac has occasionally been taxed with a fondness for 'le travaillisme britannique', he has never been in favour of nationalisation. But like de Gaulle and Pompidou, he has always seen the state as helping the economy along by a certain amount of economic planning, and has never accepted the idea that the crucial element in making a modern economy efficient is a reliance on market forces. Giscard, on the other hand, is closer to the Anglo-Saxon concept of the state as 'nightwatchman', holding the ring to ensure fair play but doing its best to keep out of the economic game for the rest of the time. It was these concepts, together with a clash of personalities between two men not noted for their readiness to see the other person's point of view, which led to Chirac's announcement, on August 26, 1976, that he was resigning as prime minister, since he 'did not think that he had the means at his disposal to assume its responsibilities effectively'.

Rumours had been in the air throughout the long, hot summer of 1976, and Chirac had in fact sent his letter of resignation to Giscard d'Estaing on July 26. It was his creation, on December 5, 1976, of the Rassemblement pour la République, a rival party to the Union pour la Démocratie Française (UDF), which gave formal expression to the two faces of French conservatism. Chirac was immediately elected president of the RPR, with 96.52 per cent of the members in favour, and followed this success by being elected as mayor of Paris, against the Giscardian Michel d'Ornano, on March 23, 1977. He was now launched on an independent political career whose obvious aim was to have himself elected president of the Republic, and he made his first attempt in 1981 when he stood against Giscard d'Estaing, and succeeded in having François Mitterrand elected.

Before then, however, two events had kept his name in the papers: the dispute in 1977 as to whether he had the right to be at one and the same time mayor of Paris and a conseiller général de la Corrèze, and the press statement which he issued from his hospital bed on November 26, 1978, after having been involved in a serious motor car accident. This statement, known as *l'appel de Cochin* from the name of the hospital where Chirac was recovering from the multiple fractures sustained when his car skidded on an icy road near the Château de Bity, his home in La Corrèze, placed him very firmly, if only temporarily, in the French Eurosceptic camp.

It was written at the suggestion of two of his advisers from whom he has now distanced himself, Pierre Juillet and Marie-France Garaud. His separation from the latter, one of the most formidable and terrifying women in French politics,[8] was apparently brought about when his wife Bernadette told him that he would have to choose between the two of them. There are a number of anecdotes suggesting that Bernadette Chirac, like Yvonne de Gaulle and Claude Pompidou, has never been very keen on seeing her husband follow a political career, and the tone of the *appel de Cochin*, with its violent denunciation of 'le parti de l'étranger qui prépare l'inféodation de la France', suggests that she was well advised to intervene in order to prevent him from continuing to play the nationalist card in his rivalry with Giscard d'Estaing, the obvious target of his wrath in November 1978.

He had, on being appointed prime minister on May 27, 1974, been required under Article 23 of the 1958 Constitution, to give up his seat as député de la Corrèze to his *suppléant*. When, after his resignation on August 28, 1976, his *suppléant* obligingly resigned – he was not obliged to do so, and there have been cases where a *suppléant* has created a certain embarrassment by not giving up the parliamentary seat which he had taken over when its holder was appointed to ministerial office – Chirac successfully stood for re-election on November 14, 1976. He was thus, on being elected mayor of Paris on March 25, 1977, already a member of parliament, and in 1970 he had been re-elected conseiller général de Meymac, a small town in La Corrèze not far from his constituency of Ussel, and where he had originally been elected to represent his fellow citizens at a local level in 1968.

It was in this capacity that he had been elected as Président du Conseil Général de la Corrèze, and in 1977, a group of socialist and communist conseillers municipaux in Paris decided that there was something not quite right about his habit of collecting elective offices as some men collect membership of golf clubs. They therefore appealed to the Conseil Constitutionnel, the body set up by the 1958 Constitution to decide, amongst other things, whether elections had been held in the correct form. They were told that there was nothing wrong with Chirac's simultaneous possession of these three elective offices, and on June 10, 1979 he added to his collection by being elected to the European Parliament as a member of the list *Intérêts de la France*.

Not even a man with the phenomenal energy of Jacques Chirac can in fact fulfil all the duties of these different offices, and he is not expected to do so. But although the day-to-day work of administering Paris is done by a team of assistants, Chirac invariably found time to reply to an extraordinarily large number of correspondents. He is, in this and other respects, every inch a politician's politician, and it is easy to imagine the frustration which he felt, both in 1981 and in 1986, when he failed to win the really big prize of president of the Republic. It was probably this frustration which explains his rather odd behaviour at the time of the 1981 presidential election, when in between the two ballots, held on April 24 and May 10, he did not tell his supporters to vote for Giscard d'Estaing. All he said was that from a personal point of view, he could do nothing but vote for him, which was very different from urging the 5,138,571 people who had voted for him to go out and vote for Giscard d'Estaing in order to keep the socialists out.

It may well be, as suggested in Chapter 3, that he was following what is known in French as *la politique du pire*: the tactic which involves making matters much worse in the short term in the hope that the catastrophe provoked may ultimately be beneficial. But if he did hope that the election of François Mitterrand would create such a crisis that he had to be called in to govern France as a neo-Gaullist saviour in a smart lounge suit, he was disappointed. All he showed was that he was a bad loser, the equivalent in the French political world of a batsman who has no scruples about making a call which would get his partner run out if this would get him an extra run or show him as the saviour of the side.

Since the president of the Fifth French Republic, at least in theory, is not supposed to be the head of a political party, Chirac had resigned as president of the RPR before the presidential election of April–May 1981. He had also given up his seat in the Assemblée Nationale, but was re-elected as député de la Corrèze in June 1981 and as president of the RPR in January 1982, after the presidential election was over. He remained, all this time, mayor of Paris, and in March 1986, having successfully defended his seat in Corrèze, was re-elected for the fourth time to the Assemblée Nationale. Although the doctrine of the separation of powers inspiring the Constitution of the Fifth Republic requires a député becoming a minister to give up his seat, Georges Pompidou remains the only prime minister not to have been elected to a seat in the Assemblée Nationale before being appointed prime minister. Once re-elected as député de la Corrèze in June 1986, and still holding office as president of the RPR, Chirac was the obvious person for François Mitterrand to ask to form a government in the then unfamiliar exercise of *la cohabitation*.

As leader of the larger of the two parties in the right-wing coalition which had just won the March 1986 legislative elections, Chirac was not only the man with the strongest right to be asked. He was also the politician who was obviously going to be the candidate of the right in the presidential election of 1988, and Mitterrand was shrewd enough see how the powers which he possessed as president could be used in order to outmanoeuvre his new prime minister at almost every turn.

Chapter 4 gives some account of how Mitterrand managed to wrong-foot Jacques Chirac between 1986 and 1988, and explains why Chirac should have insisted, when the right won the legislative elections of March 1993, that it should be Édouard Balladur and not himself who accepted the invitation to be prime minister in the second *cohabitation* with Mitterrand. Theoretically, as the phrase used in an attempt to persuade sceptical journalists that there was no rivalry between them, the two men were close friends, 'des amis de trente ans'. Both had been at the École Nationale d'Administration, and almost, though not quite, at the same time. Balladur, born on April 2, 1929, had entered l'ÉNA in 1953 but been forced to interrupt his studies for health reasons, and did not finish his studies until 1957. After military service in Algeria, where he served at his own request with a regiment of North African cavalry, the Spahis, he joined his chosen corps of the Conseil d'État in 1959.

Chirac had left at l'ÉNA in 1959, and it will be recalled that he too had served at his own request in Algeria. It would be inconceivable in France that anyone who had avoided military service in the way that Bill Clinton did should ever have a successful political career. Like Chirac, Édouard Balladur moved fairly quickly out of the civil service proper in order to go into politics, and in 1964 became adviser on social policy in Georges Pompidou's private office. He then had a successful career in private business, as manager of a company for developing the tunnel under the Mont Blanc, but came back into politics as assistant Secrétaire Général à l'Élysée when Pompidou was elected president in 1969.

This close relationship with Pompidou provides another link between Chirac and Balladur. Chirac is a very emotional man, who wept publicly on learning of Pompidou's death. Balladur, who had become general secretary at the Élysée Palace in April 1974, was there during Pompidou's final illness, and was skilful enough on the public relations front to give the impression that Pompidou was sitting in his office when in fact he was ill in hospital or at home. Pompidou appointed him executor for his will, and he went back into private business until 1980.

He then came back into politics, and when Chirac decided to see less of Pierre Juillet and Marie-France Garaud, became one of his principal advisers. Indeed, he is said to have advised Chirac not to stand against Mitterrand in 1981. On September 16, 1983, he became the first major figure openly to consider the possibility of *la cohabitation*, when he published a long article on the subject in *Le Monde*. It was not, however, until March 1986 that he faced the electorate, when he won a safe seat as an RPR candidate in Paris. This enabled him immediately to ask his *suppléant* to take his place, while he himself became Ministre de l'Économie, des Finances et de la Privatisation in Chirac's government. He was, in fact, second in the ministerial hierarchy, and the only one with the official rank of Ministre d'État (Secretary of State).

Balladur had also worked closely with Pompidou and Chirac during the events of May 1968, and in 1979 wrote a book about it called *L'Arbre de mai*. Although he was thus an experienced politician, it was in an administrative rather than an electoral context, something which made him a man whom Chirac was happy to see accepting appointment as Mitterrand's prime minister in the latter's second and final *cohabitation*. Whatever happened, Chirac thought, he would not have a serious right-wing rival in the presidential contest, and would be able to concentrate on defeating the left. But show a cat the way to the dairy, and it will soon like cream, and it was not long after beginning work as prime minister on March 29, 1993 that Balladur began to show that Chirac had, in this respect, made something of a mistake.

Balladur did not, it is true, announce his candidacy until January 18, 1995, two months after Chirac's more expected announcement on November 4, 1994. But he did so at a very good psychological moment, giving the lie to the joke about his name which Marie-France Garaud had made when she spoke in January 1994 of 'Balladur – Badamou' (Balladur the softie). She had done so after Balladur had agreed, on January 13, 1994, to withdraw a bill raising the ceiling on the amount of money local authorities were allowed to contribute to the capital costs of the écoles libres in their area. He had taken the decision after a demonstration on December 17, 1993 had brought some 700,000 people out on to the streets of Paris to defend the traditional concept of *laïcité*, and thus given the impression that he would give way every time he encountered any serious resistance to his plans.

However, on December 26, 1994, Balladur showed that he was no softie when he sent in men from the special Groupe d'Intervention de la Gendarmerie Nationale (GIGN) to free the hostages held by Islamic terrorists on an Air France Airbus at Charles de Gaulle airport. When the terrorists were all killed, causing unseemly rejoicing among the unreconstructed heathen who thought that the only good terrorist was a dead one, Balladur strengthened his position considerably in the contest against the man who was soon to add another franglais-style nickname, that of 'Battling Jacquot', to his existing appellation of 'le bulldozer'.[9]

Balladur, in contrast, offered a more reassuring image, especially for the right-wing voters who had not yet forgiven Chirac for having helped François Mitterrand to be elected in 1981. Stéphane Denis anticipated the phenomenon of his popularity early in early 1995 when he wrote in *L'Événement du jeudi* for February 2, 1992: 'De Gaulle est mort. Pompidou est mort. Chirac et Giscard ne se portent pas très bien. Mais la bourgeoisie française n'en a cure: elle n'a que Balladur en tête' (De Gaulle is dead. Pompidou is dead. Chirac and Giscard are not very well. But the French bourgeoisie is not worried: it has eyes only for Balladur).

He was, continued Denis, 'Chirac sans cheval et Giscard sans château', a reference to what Alexandre Sanguinetti is supposed to have said when he told Chirac that he was just like a cavalry officer who is given an order, dashes off to carry it out, and then come back because he has forgotten both the order and his horse. Another *énarque* and admirer of Chirac, Dominique Galouzeau de Villepin, evoked an associated but less flattering image of the French middle class when he talked about 'le balladuro-vichysme',[10] implying that Balladur would settle for the kind of quiet life which the Pétainist slogan of *Travail, Famille, Patrie* had promised the French in 1940.

The economics professor Raymond Barre, whom Valéry Giscard d'Estaing had appointed prime minister after Chirac's noisy departure in August 1976, also described Balladur in an interview with the acknowledged expert in the study of French right-wing politics, Jean Charlot, as 'une bulle suscitée par le syndrome Pétain' (a bubble produced by the Pétain syndrome). It was an odd comment to be made by a man who himself projected an even more comfortingly plump and reassuring image, but a view shared by Chirac himself. Perhaps predictably, he thought that with Balladur as prime minister, there would be 'le confort d'une tiédeur qui enliserait notre pays dans un déclin léthargique' (a comfortable lukewarm bath in which our country would sink into a comfortable lethargy).[11]

In the early months of 1995, this idea did not seem to be doing Balladur much harm. He forged comfortably ahead in the polls, helped by the fact that one of the most notorious hard men of French politics, Charles Pasqua, wrote to his former ally Chirac on January 12, 1995 to let him know that he was going to support Balladur. Lionel Jospin, chosen as the candidate of the Socialist Party on February 5, was also looking as though he might prove that Jack Lang had been quite wrong to describe him two days earlier as 'un loser, un recordman des échecs électoraux', and had the great advantage of looking financially cleaner than any other of the main candidates of the other parties.

On March 2, 1995, *Le Canard enchaîné* had revealed that Balladur had made a capital gain of 2.5 million francs by selling stock options which he had acquired while working as general manager of a large computer firm. Although there had been nothing illegal about the operation, it did not improve his image. Chirac himself was still vulnerable to the revelation, also published in *Le Canard enchaîné*, that he had benefited unduly from the grants available for the upkeep of historic buildings to have his château at Bity, in Corrèze, which he had bought in 1969 for the suspiciously low price of 200,000 francs (£20,000; $US28,000) repaired at public expense. He had, at the same time, managed to pay no taxes at all in 1971 on the grounds that he had spent large sums having his château restored.

Jospin, in contrast, (1937–; ÉNA 1963–5, corps diplomatique and professor of economics) was a Protestant. In almost every culture, membership of a minority religion tends to be associated with a higher level of both achievement and morality. French Protestants are no exception, and have made a contribution to French political life which is comparable to the enrichment of twentieth-century English literature by Catholics such as Graham Greene, David Lodge, Muriel Spark and Evelyn Waugh. They include de Gaulle's foreign secretary Maurice Couve de Murville, the socialist politicians Gaston Defferre, Georgina Dufoix, Catherine Lalumière, Michel Rocard and Catherine Trautmann as well as the current 'Premier Président de la Cour des Comptes', Pierre Joxe, son of the Gaullist politician Louis Joxe.

More than any previous contest in the Fifth Republic, the presidential election of 1995 was as much about image as about policies. As in the British general election of 1997, there was relatively little to choose between the main candidates. Lionel Jospin had as little intention as Tony Blair of implementing the traditional socialist ideas of nationalisation and increased public expenditure. Neither Chirac nor Jospin, nor for that matter Balladur, wanted to change France's foreign policy or argued that France should not join the European single currency on January 1, 1999. Although Chirac and Balladur followed de Gaulle's example in refusing to present themselves as candidates of a specific political party, everybody knew that they were both members of the Rassemblement pour la République.

Jospin's supporters talked about defending *la laïcité*, but there was no talk of a return to the potential absorption of Catholic schools in the state system implicit in Mitterrand's *grand service d'éducation laïque et unifié*. There were, it is true, differences in defence policy. Jospin was in favour of maintaining the moratorium on French nuclear tests which Mitterrand had announced in 1994, while Chirac said that there would be no more tests after one last series. Jospin said that he would like to see the period of office of the president reduced to five years, but did not make it a central plank of his campaign. While it was obvious that Chirac, and to a lesser extent Balladur, would be less inclined than Jospin to authorise regularisation of the situation of certain categories of immigrants, *les sans papiers*, none of the three main candidates supported the kind of policies which led 4,571,138 electors to vote in the first ballot, on April 23, 1995, for Jean-Marie Le Pen and the National Front policy of sending as many foreigners home as possible and restricting social benefits to those who could prove that they were ethnically French.

In the first ballot, Jospin came top, with 7,098,191, closely followed by Chirac with 6,348,696, and Balladur not far behind with 5,658,996. Robert Hue, the relatively reconstructed Communist Party candidate, received 2,632,936 votes, Arlette Laguiller, the only candidate standing for the fourth time, was rewarded with 1,615,653 for her persistence in representing the purity of the Trotskyist message. Philippe de Villiers, with his highly traditionalist Combat pour les Valeurs, received 1,443,235, and Dominique Voynet, for the ecologists, 1,010,738. Whatever de Gaulle's republic had or had not done for democracy in France, it had not discouraged what he called 'notre malheureuse propension aux divisions et aux querelles', and which others might see as an admirable diversity of opinions and enviable display of intellectual energy. Neither had it put the French off voting: 78.38 per cent of those entitled to vote turned up at the polls, and there were only 2.20 per cent spoilt papers.

Between the two rounds, Balladur behaved like a gentleman and urged everyone who had voted for him to vote for Chirac, who won by 15,763,027 votes against Jospin's 14,180,644, or 52.64 per cent against 47.36. It had been a close run thing on the first ballot, when at one stage the exit polls had suggested that it might have been Édouard Balladur and not Jacques Chirac who faced Lionel Jospin in the run-off. But Balladur gave the impression, in several senses of the word, of being too stiff and straight-laced. His extremely formal style of dress, which had given a temporary vogue to what the French think is the English custom of fastening up all three buttons on the jacket of a lounge suit, made him look like a man who was afraid to let himself go, who lacked spontaneity and drive.

Chirac, in contrast, earlier described in *The Economist* for March 26, 1988 as 'boorish and a bully', and on March 25, 1995 as having 'the reputation of an unguided missile', nevertheless looked more like a useful man to have on one's side in a tight corner. As the English philosopher, Stuart Hampshire, wrote in 1989, in an essay entitled

'Morality and Machiavelli': 'If Machiavelli returned to study modern democracies, he would be reassured to find that the great majority of voters in every democracy consistently support their government when it is successfully aggressive in face of foreign powers'.[12]

It is a remark which explains the success of Ronald Reagan and Margaret Thatcher, and which accounts for much of the attraction which Jacques Chirac's image had for the French voters of 1995. France might not have any enemies right then, but you never knew. One of the most impressive attributes of the president of the Fifth French Republic is his possession of the code for the French nuclear deterrent. The voters of 1995 were not afraid to put Chirac's finger on the button. It is fortunate that the only major mistake which he has so far made has concerned the timing of an election.

1995–7

On May 18, 1995, Chirac appointed as prime minister one of his closest and most experienced political colleagues, Alain Juppé, who was just 50. Like Chirac, Juppé had been at the École Nationale d'Administration, and like Georges Pompidou had also been a student at the École Normale Supérieure de la rue d'Ulm. In 1972, he became a member of the same *corps* as Giscard d'Estaing, the Inspection des Finances, but in 1978 had himself *mis en disponibilité* in order to become a member of Chirac's team for administering Paris. In 1982, he became financial director for the whole city. In 1986, he was elected as an RPR député for one of the Paris constituencies, and between 1986 and 1988 was official spokesman for the government which Chirac formed under François Mitterrand.

At the same time, Alain Juppé was also a member of the European Parliament, keeping until 1989 the seat which he had first won in 1984. He served as foreign minister under Édouard Balladur between 1993 and 1995, and in June 1995 was elected mayor of Bordeaux. Between 1988 and 1993, he had been general secretary of the Rassemblement pour la République. In 1995, when Chirac resigned in order to observe the convention that candidates for the presidency do not run on a party ticket, he became its president. Like Chirac's own career, Alain Juppé's epitomised a central aspect of the Fifth Republic, its reliance on highly trained technocrats who move with impressive ease from one post to another, and combine in their own person responsibilities which in other political cultures would be spread out among at least half a dozen people.

It may, in this respect, have been partly Juppé's fault that the right lost the legislative elections of May–June 1977. He had a high opinion of himself, and did not hesitate to show it. In December 1995, at the height of the public sector strikes which paralysed France for three weeks in the run-up to Christmas, he was interviewed on television by a group of journalists who tried every device imaginable to make him pronounce the word 'négociation'. He steadfastly refused, though was more forthcoming on his own achievements. When asked whether it was true that he had been 'un bon élève' at school, he replied: 'Non. J'étais un excellent élève'.

On other matters, however, he reminded many of those watching him of the definition of an *énarque* given by the professional clown Coluche, who stood for election as president of the Republic in 1981, but is perhaps better remembered for having established *les restaurants du coeur*, where anybody really down on their luck can go and eat for nothing. An *énarque*, he said, is someone who, when you ask him a question, makes you forget what it was by the time he finishes answering it, and this was exactly what Juppé did. Had Balladur been appointed prime minister, he might have given way with better grace, which was what Juppé finally had to do anyway, and his failure to carry out the proposed reforms which caused the strikes in November–December 1995 summarises the difficulties likely to be faced by any government in France, whether of left or right.

The most important of these is the deficit in the social security budget. Except for the special tax created in 1991, *la contribution sociale généralisée*, all the money for medical payments, state-funded old age pensions, family allowances, accidents at work and unemployment payments is provided by the compulsory contributions paid by employers and employees. The fact that the system was established in October 1945 renders any proposed reforms vulnerable to the objection 'Vous n'allez pas toucher à ce qui a été créé par le général de Gaulle', and the French are understandably attached to what are widely and accurately referred to as 'les avantages acquis'.

The system has, however, been more or less in deficit since the mid-1950s, and by 1995 this deficit had risen to 230 milliards francs, the equivalent of 4 per cent of the Gross Domestic Product. Medical expenditure in France per head of the population is the fourth highest in the world, immediately after that of the United States of America, Canada and Switzerland, and accounts for 10 per cent of the Gross Domestic Product. There is little that any politician can do to change deeply rooted personal habits, but the plan put forward by Alain Juppé in November 1995 did try to make it more expensive to visit the doctor, in particular by putting an end to what is called *le nomadisme médical*, the possibility for a patient to consult several doctors, and be reimbursed for 75 per cent of the cost of each consultation, if she or he does not like the diagnosis and remedies initially suggested.

More importantly, *le plan Juppé* sought to impose a parliamentary control over the joint councils of trade union and patients' representatives responsible for running the finances of the social security system. He also tried to require civil servants to have worked forty years, instead of thirty-seven and a half, before becoming eligible for a full pension, and ought to have taken account of the shot across the bows of any politician trying to reduce *les avantages acquis des fonctionnaires* in what had happened a few months earlier to Alain Madelin (1946–), the son of an industrial worker who had been a member of the Communist Party, but whose own political career had begun in the extreme right-wing group known as *Occident*.

Perhaps because Madelin, unlike Juppé, did not go the École Nationale d'Administration, he is one of the few leading French politicians to share something of the enthusiasm for market forces characteristic of Margaret Thatcher and Ronald Reagan. He was minister for industry in Chirac's government between 1986 and 1988, and had been appointed Ministre de l'Économie et des Finances in Alain Juppé's government in May 1995. On August 24, 1995, however, he made a speech criticising the privileges enjoyed by French civil servants. On August 25 he was compelled to resign.

The strikes provoked by the publication of Alain Juppé's proposed reform of the social security system were almost entirely confined to the public sector. They were accompanied by a series of demonstrations, of which the largest, on December 12, 1995, had brought over 2 million people out onto the streets of Paris and the provinces. There are clearly limits to what any government can do to deprive people of social advantages which they already possess, especially in a country with as long a history of street protests as France, and as powerfully organised a public sector. French trade unions, it is true, may be among the weakest in Europe, with only 10 per cent of the total work force as members. But as the action of the lorry drivers showed in the spring of 1996, and again in November 1997, you do not need many discontented but determined employees to bring the country to a standstill, especially if the strikers enjoy a measure of public sympathy.

One of the paradoxes of French political culture, as well as one of the most striking examples of what the French like to call *l'exception française*, lies in the contrast between a state which gives every appearance of being as strong as its British or American counterparts, or perhaps even stronger, and its extreme vulnerability to sectorial pressure. Another is the fact that the reforms most eagerly wished for by one political grouping are sometimes more effectively carried out by the party which one might have thought opposed to them. This happened most dramatically when Charles de Gaulle gave Algeria the independence which only a few left-wing journalists in the France of the 1950s had wished to see granted, and may be about to happen with the economic and social policies being implemented by Lionel Jospin.

These are not, with the exception of the proposed reduction of the working week from thirty-nine to thirty-five hours, particularly socialistic. He has, it is true, pleased the ecologists by abandoning the proposed Superphénix nuclear generator. He has also, as he said he would, been more generous in regularising the situation of *les sans papiers*, and has defied both the Front National and sectors of the traditional right by reaffirming the principle of the *droit du sol* over that of the *droit du sang* as far as the procedure for obtaining French citizenship is concerned. It will, so long as his party stays in power, be enough to be born in France, whatever the nationality of one's parents, and to have lived for five years in France, to have the automatic right to French citizenship at the age of 18.

In other areas, however, he has not acted in a way which is notably different from that of a right-wing prime minister with a greater gift for public relations than Alain Juppé. He has reduced public spending by 10 milliards, brought the public deficit down to the 3 per cent required by the Maastricht criteria, increased the minimum wage by only 4 per cent, half of that demanded by the trade unions, and is talking about a reform the social security system which is very similar to the one proposed by Alain Juppé in 1995. In spite of the promises made by certain socialists during the election campaign, he has not leaned upon the now privately-owned Renault car company to keep its factory open at Vilvordes, in Belgium. More particularly, he refused on January 21, 1998, to grant any substantial increase in benefits for the unemployed.

He has not, however, managed to bring about a significant reduction in the number of people unemployed. This remains in the region of 12 per cent of the labour force, below the 20 per cent in Spain, but depressingly higher than the 6 per cent in Great Britain, the 3.5 per cent in the United States and the 2 per cent in Japan. The persistence of high unemployment after the presidential election of 1995, especially after the frequency with which Jacques Chirac had promised to give absolute priority to reducing 'la fracture sociale' and 'l'exclusion' which unemployment produces, was one of the main reasons for the defeat of the RPR in the May–June 1997 elections. But there were other factors, of which the 15.24 per cent vote for the Front National was one of the most important.

An article in *Le Monde* for June 3, 1997 by its editor, Jean-Pierre Colombani, made a more precise link between the size of the Front National vote and the decline in popularity of the RPR. Traditionally, it argued, Gaullism has based much of its appeal on its ability to defeat political extremes, whether these took a right-wing form, as in the Vichy régime of 1940–4, the support for L'Algérie Française, and the terrorism orchestrated by the Organisation de l'Armée Secrète after 1962, or the left-wing form of the French Communist Party or the student rebels of 1968. But it was now failing to contain the threat of a right-wing fascism represented by the Front National, with the result that more voters were turning to the Socialist Party as a possible barrier against Jean-Marie Le Pen.

This was not necessarily a criticism of Chirac himself, whose popularity in the public opinion polls contrasts sharply with the decline in the fortunes of the RPR. A major change which he introduced into French politics, immediately after his election as president, was a different attitude towards the Vichy régime. For de Gaulle, this had never been anything but an illegal interlude, a minority régime supported solely by a handful of totally unrepresentative Frenchmen. Georges Pompidou took a similar attitude, giving priority to the healing of wounds and national reconciliation. So, too, did Valéry Giscard d'Estaing, while François Mitterrand had laid a wreath on the tomb of Marshal Pétain and said that the Republic could in no way be held responsible for the crimes committed by the Vichy régime.

Chirac, in contrast, took the opportunity of a meeting held on July 17, 1995 to commemorate the fifty-third anniversary of 'la rafle du Vél' d'hiv' to declare with a total lack of ambiguity that 'la folie criminelle de l'occupant a été secondée par l'État français'. He thus made it impossible to deny that when, on July 17, 1943, thousands of Jews were rounded up, and parked in appalling conditions in an arena originally built to house indoor bicycle races, before being sent off to the extermination camps, it was also the fault of the French government of the time.

What the electors who sent back a left-wing majority to the Assemblée Nationale were also saying was that they did not care for a situation in which all the elective powers in the Republic were under the control of the same political grouping. For in 1997, the right had a majority not only in the National Assembly but also in the Senate, and in most of the *conseils régionaux* and *conseils généraux*. This did not, if one follows the convention of seeing the electorate as a single body with one collective mind, seem altogether a good idea to the French. De Gaulle, after all, had always seen the president as an arbiter standing apart from as well as above the different bodies which exercised authority in the state. He was not, at least in theory, to be a party leader, and in depriving Jacques Chirac of his parliamentary majority the electors of May–June 1997 were giving reality to this particular concept of the presidency. It might, at first sight, seem strange to have as head of state the leader of the parliamentary opposition. But if he were to separate himself more clearly from all political parties, there might be a good case for having as president a politician who is genuinely the guardian of the welfare of the whole nation.

6 Conclusion

The epigram that 'History is about chaps' does not involve the acceptance of the theory of Thomas Carlyle (1795–1881) that the crucial events in history are the result of the role played by great heroes. There is no evidence that even de Gaulle thought that this was the case. But neither did he accept the idea that history is about general economic and social trends over which individuals can exercise no influence.

It is a notion put forward at some length by Tolstoy in *War and Peace* (1865–9), and which lay behind the vulgarised Marxism of Georgi Plekhanov (1856–1918). Plekhanov's insistence on the need for Russia to go through the process of capitalist industrialisation before achieving socialism led him to support the Menshevik faction against Lenin, whose actions in 1917 were based on the more voluntarist conception of history which Marx expressed when he wrote in his eighth thesis on Feuerbach that 'philosophers in the past have tried only to understand history. Our task is to change it'.

Although there is no necessary incompatibility between the approach to history which concentrates on the role played by certain individuals, and the emphasis placed on long-term economic and social trends, both raise the same philosophical problem: are these trends so irresistible that even the most determined and prestigious individual can exercise no influence on them at all? Or is it true, in the last resort, that men are masters of their fate, and that it is the decisions taken by individuals which are ultimately decisive?

Like all philosophical questions, it is essentially unanswerable. But it would be a poor reaction to the complexity of historical events if historians refrained even from asking it. The two main events of the period which began in 1958 with the return to power of Charles de Gaulle are the winning of the Cold War and the final disappearance of the belief that the way to a more efficient as well as a more just society lies through the public ownership of the means of production, distribution and exchange. These events touch the whole of the industrialised world. The ending of French colonialism, important though it remains for Europe and North Africa, is not on the same scale.

It is easy to argue, especially from a point of view as conservative as my own, that the winning of the Cold War was due to a series of actions taken by specific individuals. These include the proclamation by Dean Acheson of the Truman Doctrine on March 21, 1947, the decision by President Truman to defy the Soviet blockade of Berlin by the airlift of June 1948–May 1949, his immediate reaction to the invasion of Korea on June 24, 1950 by the despatch of American forces under the flag of the United Nations, the refusal of Presidents Eisenhower and Kennedy, between November 1958 and October 1961, to accept the proposed transformation of West Berlin into the 'Free City' proposed by Mr Krushchev, the blockade of Cuba in October 1962 and the subsequent withdrawal of the Soviet missiles, and the re-armament programme of President Reagan which finally led to the collapse of the Soviet economy. Without any one of these actions by these individuals, the outcome of the struggle between the Soviet Union and the West might have been very different.

The two events with which this book is principally concerned, the end of the socialist dream and the abandonment of French North Africa, nevertheless now seem so inevitable that the history of France between 1958 and 1997 looks at first sight like an almost text-book illustration of the Tolstoy-Plekhanov hypothesis. On the other hand, however, each event was so closely associated with one man that it is hard to think of it as being as totally immune to human control as the wind which bloweth where it listeth. François Mitterrand was not a believer in whole-scale nationalisation. But if the policy adopted under his direction between 1981 and 1983 had succeeded, it would now no longer seem so self-evident that the market economy had proved its superiority over socialist planning. Somebody had to carry out one last experiment in socialism in a major industrialised country to show that it was not the best way of organising a modern European society. If Mitterrand had not been there to try, we might still not know. Even if an individual is only a catalyst, it is worth while looking at what it was that he did which made the situation crystallise. When, from March 1983 onwards, Mitterrand connived in the rebirth of French capitalism, he also acted in a way which few socialist politicians could have emulated.

Charles de Gaulle may or may not have become president in 1958 with the aim of keeping Algeria French. But he, if anyone, had the formal powers and personal prestige to try to do so, and the remarks which he made about his reluctance to carry out the policy he finally adopted suggest that he would not have been unhappy to fulfil the ambitions of the men who brought him back to power. The fact that he decided to make France leave Algeria consequently underlines the limits to the influence any one man can exercise over a general trend such as the end of European hegemony in North Africa. At the same time, it is a reminder of something even more important: that if de Gaulle had not been there to make other people recognise the inevitability of this trend, a war might have been fought within the borders of France itself, a war whose uncertain outcome would have shown that the only inevitability in human affairs is the one born of the unpredictability inseparable from the clash of arms.

Appendix A
French régimes from 1792 to 1958

The first French Republic came into being on September 21, 1792. It lasted, officially, until May 18, 1804, when Napoleon Bonaparte proclaimed himself Empereur des Français, thus inaugurating the First Empire, with himself as Napoleon I. The First French Empire came to an end with the abdication of Napoleon I on April 6, 1814. It was succeeded by the Restoration Monarchy, until this was overthrown by the revolution of July 1830. There then followed the July Monarchy, with the Orleanist Louis-Philippe as king. This lasted until February 25, 1848, when it was replaced by the Second Republic.

On December 10, 1848, Louis Napoleon Bonaparte, nephew of Napoleon I, was elected president of the Second Republic. On December 2, 1851, he carried out a *coup d'état* which suspended the Constitution, which had initially entitled him to be president only for four years. On December 21, he had himself elected for ten years, and on December 2, 1852, by another *coup d'état*, proclaimed himself emperor under the title of Napoleon III. The Second Empire which he thus created lasted from December 2, 1852 to September 4, 1870, when the defeat of France in the Franco–Prussian war led to the proclamation of the Third Republic. On July 10, 1940, the Third Republic was replaced, by a vote of 569 to 80 in the National Assembly, by what was officially known as L'État Français, but which is more commonly referred to as 'le régime de Vichy'. On October 27, 1946, this was replaced by the Fourth Republic.

The Fourth Republic fell as a result of a military uprising in Algeria on May 13, 1958 which brought de Gaulle to power.

Appendix B
Prime ministers of the Fifth Republic

Note: Prime ministers, being civil servants, indication is given of the *corps* to which they belonged (see Appendix C).

1 Michel Debré (1912–96), January 1959–April 1962. Conseil d'État.

2 Georges Pompidou (July 5, 1911–April 2, 1974), April 13, 1962–July 10, 1968. Corps de L'Éducation Nationale, Conseil d'État.

3 Maurice Couve de Murville (January 24, 1907–), July 21, 1968–June 16, 1969. Inspection des Finances, Ambassadeur de France, Corps diplomatique.

4 Jacques Chaban-Delmas (March 7, 1915–), June 20, 1969–July 5, 1972. Inspection des Finances.

5 Pierre Messmer (March 20, 1916–), July 7, 1972–May 27, 1974. Administrateur des colonies.

6 Jacques Chirac (November 29, 1932–), (a) May 27, 1974–August 25, 1976; (b) March 20, 1986–May 9, 1988. Cour des Comptes, ancien élève de L'École Nationale d'Administration.

7 Raymond Barre (April 4, 1924–), August 27, 1976–May 13, 1981. Professeur d'Économie politique, Corps de l'Éducation Nationale.

8 Pierre Mauroy (July 5, 1928–), May 22, 1981–July 16, 1984. Syndicaliste et homme politique.

9 Laurent Fabius (August 20, 1946–), July 17, 1984–May 1988. Conseil d'État, ancien élève de L'École Nationale d'Administration.

10 Michel Rocard (August 23, 1930–), May 10, 1988–May 15, 1991. Inspection des Finances, ancien élève de L'École Nationale d'Administration.

11   Édith Cresson (January 23, 1934–), May 15, 1991–April 2, 1992. Diplômée des Hautes Études Commerciales, Docteur en droit, femme politique.

12   Pierre Bérégovoy (December 23, 1925–May 1, 1993), April 2, 1992–March 28, 1993. Certificat d'aptitude professionnelle d'ajusteur (trained fitter), diplômé de l'École d'organisation scientifique du travail, homme politique.

13   Édouard Balladur (May 2, 1929–), March 29, 1993–May 9, 1995. Conseil d'État, ancien élève de L'École Nationale d'Administration.

14   Alain Juppé (August 15, 1945–), May 10, 1995–May, 1997. Inspection des Finances, ancien élève de L'École Nationale d'Administration.

15   Lionel Jospin (July 12, 1937–), May 1997–. Secrétaire au Ministère des Affaires Étrangères (Corps diplomatique et consulaire), ancien élève de L'École Nationale d'Administration.

Appendix C
A note on the French civil service

Each French civil servant belongs to a corps, of which there are over 600. It is the corps which pays his or her salary, and constitutes the basis of his or her official identity. There are technical corps, such as le corps des ponts et chaussées, to which access is through the oldest of the Grandes Écoles, l'École des Ponts et Chaussées, created in 1754, and administrative corps, of which the largest is le corps des administrateurs civils, modelled on the British administrative class.

Since teachers in the state sector are civil servants, they make up the largest of all the corps, le corps de l'Éducation Nationale. This itself is divided into le corps des professeurs et maîtres de conférences (for universities); le corps de agrégés et certifiés (for teachers in secondary schools); and the largest, le corps des instituteurs (for primary schools, soon to be renamed as le corps des professeurs de l'enseignement primaire). Raymond Barre was a member of the corps de professeurs et maîtres de conférence; Georges Pompidou of the corps des agrégés et certifiés; his father, Léon, of the corps des instituteurs.

The three most prestigious corps, known as les Grands Corps de l'État, are le Conseil d'État, la Cour des Comptes, and l'Inspection des Finances. The nearest equivalent to the Cour des Comptes in the British system is the National Audit Office, the head of which is the Controller and Auditor General. However, whereas in the United Kingdom the Controller and Auditor General is responsible to parliament, the Cour des Comptes is an independent body. Its members *ont le statut de magistrat* (are judges), and have the legal power to check all public accounts in order to see that the money voted by parliament has been used both as parliament wished and in the most efficient way possible; and to take action against civil servants found to be in default. Its members include Jacques Chirac, who officially retired in 1997, on reaching the age of 65.

Le Conseil d'État is the supreme body for administrative law, which in France is separate from both the ordinary civil law and the criminal law. When Georges Pompidou joined the Conseil d'État in 1946, he left the corps de l'Éducation Nationale, which is too conscious of its status to allow its members the traditional *détachement de leur corps d'origine*. Members of the Inspection des Finances, of which both Valéry Giscard d'Estaing and Michel Rocard are members, are despatched to other ministries in order to check on the way public money is being spent, and, more importantly, to advise on the best financial techniques to be used for attaining their targets.

Most members of les Grands Corps de l'État are former students of the École Nationale d'Administration, established in 1945 to train senior civil servants, and set up by joint agreement between the Gaullist Michel Debré and the communist leader Maurice Thorez, who had recently returned to France from Moscow, where he had spent the war. It is a postgraduate school, and entry is by a very competitive examination (*concours*), in which there are normally thirty candidates for every place. The first year of the two-and-a-half year course is spent working in the public sector, generally in a Préfecture or sous-préfecture. Although the École Nationale d'Administration 'ne délivre pas de diplôme', is not a degree-granting institution, the final examination is *un concours*, and names are published in order of merit. Students arriving in *la botte*, the first fifteen to twenty out of a total intake of 100, traditionally choose one of the Grands Corps de État.

Although there is a tendency for former pupils of the École Nationale d'Administration (l'ÉNA) to be enlightened moderates, not all of them conform to this particular ideological mode quite so neatly as two of Mitterrand's prime ministers, Laurent Fabius (Conseil d'État) and Michel Rocard, who on coming first (*major*) in the *concours de sortie*, chose L'Inspection des Finances. Philippe Séguin, one of the most vigorous figures on the right wing of the main conservative party in France, Jacques Chirac's Rassemblement pour la République, is an *ancien élève de l'ÉNA*, and member of la Cour des Comptes. Philippe de Villiers, who stood in the presidential election of 1995 as a candidate of the highly traditional Catholic right and Jean-Pierre Chèvenement, one of the most left-wing members of the Socialist Party are both former pupils of l'ÉNA. So, too, is Yvon Blot, a member of the central committee of Jean-Marie Le Pen's Front National. Lionel Jospin was a pupil at l'ÉNA at the same time as the man elected in December 1997 to be head of the major French employers' organisation, the Conseil National du Patronat Français (CNPF), the immensely rich Baron Ernest-Antoine Seillière de Laborde. Although the two men are said to be quite close friends,

Seillière de Laborde has taken upon himself what he frequently presents as the quasi sacred mission of opposing one of Jospin's main projects for reducing unemployment, the reduction of the working week from thirty-nine to thirty-five hours.

French civil servants can obtain *une mise en détachement* in order to go and work in another ministry, another sector of the public service, or a state-owned company. They retain their pension rights, and can go back to their *corps d'origine*, without loss of seniority, *sans perte d'ancienneté*, rejoining it at the rank which they would have reached by the automatic promotion system. They can also, if the head of their corps agrees, obtain what is officially know as *une mise en disponibilité pour convenance personnelle* (unpaid leave, with the possibility of rejoining the service at will, though with no guarantee of promotion). The frequency with which French civil servants use the safety net provided by the *mise en disponibilité* system in order to go into politics, whether as advisers to ministers or active politicians in their own right, is a major factor explaining the role played by career civil servants in national as well as local politics.

The system is not seen as a threat to the ideological plurality which is an essential part of a system of democratic government. The French may talk ironically about *la nomenklatura*, especially when discussing the role played by former students from the École Nationale d'Administration, but there is no resemblance to the system which existed in the former Soviet Union. The fact that civil servants obtaining *une mise en disponibilité* in order to enter politics work for a wide variety of political parties nevertheless evokes some of the ideas of the now largely forgotten American sociologist, James Burnham (1905–87).

Burnham's most influential book, *The Managerial Revolution*, was published in 1941. It argued that modern society, whether in a capitalist or a communist form, had come to be governed by a new class which owed its power solely to its technical expertise. This class was replacing the old individualist, capitalist entrepreneur, with a consequent divorce between ownership and control. All that the managers owned, at least initially, was their skill. This class was also politically neutral, in that it was prepared to serve any régime which enabled it to conserve its privileges. It was, Burnham argued, likely to remain the dominant class for a long time, since its policy of open recruitment enabled it to absorb the ambitious and intelligent who might otherwise call its position into question.

For a number of reasons, Burnham is rarely mentioned in contemporary analyses of late capitalist society. One of these is that he made the mistake of issuing a number of more specific prophecies which proved wrong. As George Orwell pointed out in 1946 in 'James Burnham and the managerial revolution', he predicted in 1941 that Germany and Japan would win the second world war, and then in 1944 that Russia would soon dominate the whole of Eurasia (*The Collected Essays, Journalism and Letters of George Orwell*, vol. IV, London, Secker and Warburg, 1968, pp. 160–81). It is also possible that the description of the 'inner party' in *Nineteen Eighty-Four* is based at least partly on Burnham's concept of the new class of professional managers.

Burnham may also, however, owe the infrequency with which he is now mentioned to the fact that he did, very broadly, get it right. The position in French society of the *énarques*, the former pupils of the École Nationale d'Administration, is a specific illustration of his thesis. There is, naturally, no question of their using violence or fraud to acquire or retain their privileges, and in this respect are totally unlike the members of the 'inner party' in Orwell's Eurasia. When, as frequently happens, they decide to give their power a greater legitimacy by standing for election, they do so in a fair and open system, and are generally successful. But they do constitute a particular class, and one which is equally conscious of its responsibilities and determined to retain its privileges.

They are extremely skilful. They are recruited by open competition. The *annuaire des anciens élèves de l'ÉNA*, which publishes the address, telephone number and current occupation of each former pupil, enables them to remain very easily in contact with one another, and they are relatively few in number. As an article entitled 'France's durable élite', published in *The Economist* on August 9, 1997 pointed out, there are only 5,000 living *énarques*, as compared to 100,000 Oxbridge graduates in British society, and an even higher number of former pupils from the Ivy League universities in the United States. Although only 2 per cent of *énarques* take up a political career, those that do so prove very successful. As Appendix B points out, six of the fifteen prime ministers of the Fifth Republic went to l'ÉNA.

Foreign though this system is to Anglo-Saxon concepts of the separation of powers and the idea of a politically neutral civil service, comparable arrangements used to exist in Italy. However, in 1997, new rules were introduced requiring civil servants standing for election to resign at least six months in advance. A German civil servant who accepts a post which is deemed to be highly political, such as a Staatssekretar, the equivalent of the British permanent secretary, forfeits both tenure and pension rights. The role played by civil servants in national politics can thus be seen as a further example of what the French like to call *l'exception française*, especially since some 40 per cent of the current members of the Assemblée Nationale are also civil servants *en disponibilité*. Another 40 per cent are *des salariés* (paid employees) from private sector firms, who are required by law to grant their employees leave of absence to stand for election, either at a local or at a national level. They then have to take these employees back if they are not elected, or if they decide, on completing a political career, that they would prefer to resume their earlier calling.

Notes

Introduction

1 See Dominique Frémy, *Quid des Présidents de la République et des candi-dats*, Robert Laffont, Paris, 1987, p. 17 and p. 48. This invaluable volume will henceforth be referred to as Frémy – *Quid*. See the Bibliography for details of the books published by de Gaulle, Pompidou, Giscard d'Estaing, Mitterrand and Chirac.
2 Frémy – *Quid*, p. 426.

1 Charles de Gaulle: the founding father

1 The matter is discussed in more detail in my *French Caesarism from Napoleon I to Charles de Gaulle*, Macmillan, London, 1989. This studies the pattern which began in 1799, when Napoleon I put an end to the chaos left behind by the revolution of 1789, and which was continued by his nephew, Louis Napoleon, who seized power in response to a less obvious crisis in 1852. It was further illustrated by the fact that in 1940, it was also to a soldier, the 84-year-old Marshal Pétain, that the French chose to entrust the government of their country in the worst disaster ever to afflict them.
2 See J.-B. Duroselle, *L'Abîme, 1939–1945*, Politique étrangère de l'Imprimerie Nationale de France, Paris, 1982, p. 443.
3 Pierre Mendès France, *La Vérité guidait leurs pas*, Gallimard, Paris, 1976, pp. 55–6.
4 See Jean Lacouture, *Le Rebelle*, Seuil, 1984, p. 159, who attributes it to their 'imbecility' and earlier (pp. 16–120) gives a very favourable portrait of de Gaulle.
5 *Le Fil de l'Épée*, Paris, 1932 (Plon, 1971), p. 100.
6 On November 12, 1971, the extreme right-wing journal *Minute* was delighted to pick up this point in its review.
7 Frémy – *Quid*, p. 433.
8 *C'était de Gaulle*, p. 55 and p. 159.
9 *Candide*, Chapter IV.
10 Peyrefitte, *C'était de Gaulle*, p. 388.
11 *C'était de Gaulle*, p. 307.

12 For a discussion of the meaning of these terms, see Philip Thody *An Historical Introduction to the European Union*, Routledge, 1997.
13 Frémy – *Quid*, p 435.
14 *Le Souverain*, Éditions du Seuil, Paris, 1986, p. 636.

2 Georges Pompidou: the conscientious uncle

1 Christine Clerc, *Jacques, Édouard, Charles, Philippe et les autres*, Albin Michel, 1994, Collection 'J'ai lu', p. 47.
2 *L'Élan du coeur*, Plon, Paris, 1997, p. 104.
3 Although the denial comes from Pompidou himself in his *Pour rétablir une vérité*, p. 33, his widow Claude repeats it on p. 109 of her autobiography, *L'élan du coeur*, Plon, Paris, 1997, albeit in the form 'quelqu'un sachant écrire'.
4 Georges Pompidou, *Pour rétablir une vérité*, Flammarion, Paris, 1982, p. 277.
5 For more details, see Appendix C.
6 Figures taken from pp. 742–4 of the 1998 *Quid*.
7 See Jacques Massu, *Baden 68*, Plon, Paris, 1983.
8 There is a detailed account of events in Éric Roussel, *Georges Pompidou, Le Président d'avant la crise*, pp. 277–320, Jean-Claude Lattès, Paris, 1984.
9 De Gaulle's insistence on 'finding something for Couve' went back to 1943, and may be explained by the respect he felt for civil servants who had risen in the service in the same conventional way as he had achieved promotion in the army. Although it was he himself who arranged in 1946 for Pompidou to become a member of the Conseil d'État by what is known as the 'tour extérieur', appointment from outside, de Gaulle managed to forget this and remained convinced that Pompidou had been successful in the open competition which is the normal mode of entry. That was how Couve de Murville had become a member of the Inspection des Finances in 1932, and which, in addition to his readiness to do whatever he was told without the arguments which sometimes characterised Pompidou's attitude, gave him such prestige in de Gaulle's eyes.
   The anecdote most frequently quoted to illustrate both de Gaulle's suspicion of the home-grown resistance movement and his respect for those who had risen in the service 'par la voie hiérarchique et le tableau d'avancement' concerns his inspection in 1944 of a group from Les Forces Françaises de l'Intérieur (FFI). After being introduced to 'le colonel Machin', 'le commandant Dupont', 'le capitaine Dufour' and 'le lieutenant Barattin', de Gaulle found himself face to face with 'le soldat 2e classe Bardamu'. 'Alors' he said, noticing the absence from his uniform of any badges of rank, 'Vous ne savez même pas coudre?' (So, you don't even know how to sew?).
10 Georges Pompidou, *Pour rétablir une vérité*, Flammarion, Paris, 1982, p. 199.
11 See Christine Clerc, *Jacques, Édouard, Charles, Philippe et les autres*, Albin Michel, 1994, Collection 'J'ai lu', pp. 50–1.
12 *Les Gaullistes*, 1963, p. 53: Madame de Gaulle 'a écarté sans pitié de l'entourage tout divorcé ou divorcée, rayé volontiers sur les listes des réceptions intimes les couples unis civilement, battu froid ceux qui

tombaient sous le soupçon de libertinage'. It will be recalled that since the separation of Church and state in 1905, the only legally valid marriage ceremony in France is the one conducted by the representative of the Republic, the mayor. Madame de Gaulle was not alone at the time in regarding any marriage not subsequently blessed by the Church as merely a convenient arrangement for living in sin. For her to have invited the Pompidous the moment the rumours began circulating would have been enough to kill them stone dead.

13 A succinct account of 'l'affaire Marcovitch' can be found on p. 508 of Frémy – *Quid*.

3 Valéry Giscard d'Estaing: the ambitious nephew

1 Frédéric Abadie and Jean-Pierre Corcelette, *Valéry Giscard d'Estaing*, Balland, Paris, 1997, p. 16.

2 Frémy – *Quid*, pp. 138–9.

3 See *The Collected Essays, Journalism and Letters of George Orwell*, vol. I, Secker and Warburg, London, 1968, pp. 460–93.

4 See Appendix B, Prime ministers of the Fifth Republic, in this volume. For other aspects of Giscard d'Estaing's career, see Appendix C, A note on the French civil service.

5 See *The Bonfire of the Vanities*, 1987, Picador, London, 1988, pp. 70 and 75. Uncharacteristically Wolfe makes a mistakes in referring on p. 75 to Giscard d'Estaing as the French president. He was, at the time when the loan was launched, finance minister.

6 See *Quid* for 1991, p. 1946. For details of the workings of the system whereby the French pay tax in three annual lump sums, see Thody and Evans, *Faux Amis and Key Words*, Athlone, London, 1985, p. 108. It is often said that the French state relies much less on direct than on indirect taxation, and Michel Jobert (1921–), a former student at l'ÉNA, and a member of the Cour des Comptes who served as a former minister both under Pompidou and François Mitterrand, is quoted on p. 2076 of *Quid* for 1996 as saying that over half of those liable to tax in France do not pay income tax ('déjà, de nombreux contribuables (environ 50 per cent en 1986) ne le paient plus'). However, international comparisons of the amount of money which the state deducts directly from individuals are to be treated with caution. According to an article in *The Economist* for December 6, the average income tax rate for a married man earning $60,000 a year in 1997 was 35 per cent in Italy, 34 per cent in Germany and Canada, 29 per cent in Britain, 27 per cent in France, 26 per cent in Japan and 25 per cent in the United States. However, this figure includes social security contributions, which are much higher in France than in the UK.

7 For a more detailed account of the early obstacles put in the path of the implementation of the 'loi Neuwirth', see the article from *L'Express* for December 18, 1972 in *Les Cahiers de l'Express*, mai 1968–mai 1993, no. 21.

On December 18, 1997, *France-Inter* devoted several programmes to the fortieth anniversary of Lucien Neuwirth's introduction of his bill before the Chambre des députés. He explained in an interview how de Gaulle, a practising Catholic who once said that he would like to see the population of France rise to 100 million, had initially opposed his idea, remarking as he did so 'Nous n'allons pas livrer la France à la bagatelle' (We are not going to make France a haven for free love). He did, however, agree to receive Neuwirth at la Boisserie, and needed only an hour to be persuaded to withdraw his opposition. The decisive argument used by Neuwirth was that since it was he, de Gaulle, who had given women the vote in 1945, it was reasonable for him also to give them the choice as to when to have children. De Gaulle, Neuwirth explained, was essentially a pragmatist, and was also sufficiently intelligent not to make the confusion which was common in some conservative and Catholic circles in France at the time between contraception and abortion.

8 *France in the Giscard Presidency*, Allen and Unwin, London, 1981, pp. 188–9. This excellent book is now, unfortunately, out of print. It nevertheless remains one of the best studies of twentieth-century French politics, either in French or English.

9 Published by Fayard. Although only 200,000 copies were originally printed, it sold over a million and a half in all. The royalties went to establish the Fondation Anne-Aymone Giscard d'Estaing for children in need.

The tradition whereby the president's wife concerns herself primarily with good works goes back to La Maréchale Mac-Mahon whose husband was President from 1873 to 1879. She was president of the central committee for the Red Cross in France, and gave 10,000 francs a month to charity, a figure which caused consternation to her successor Madame Grévy, who was more careful with her pennies. In 1889, Madame Carnot began the custom whereby a collection was made every Christmas at the Élysée for children in need. President Faure's daughter Lucie, a somewhat formidable lady, also concerned herself with children in need, establishing in 1899 La Ligue Fraternelle des Enfants de France. Madame Poincaré put the manuscript of her husband's *Mémoires* on sale for a children's charity, while La Maréchale Pétain concerned herself particularly with the distribution of baby clothes. Bernadette Chirac, in addition to being conseillère générale de la Corrèze, is also Présidente de la fondation Hôpitaux de Paris, and of the Fédération du Pont Neuf, an organisation devoted to encouraging student exchanges between Western Europe and the former Soviet empire.

10 Frémy – *Quid*, p. 540. On p. 474 of *The Age of Extremes*, Abacus, London, 1995, Eric Hobsbawm gives the average price in late 1981 as $41 a barrel. He is, nevertheless, fairly representative of left-wing historians in being fairly coy (on p. 245) as to why the Arab states increased the price of oil, and sees Israel (p. 220) as a colonising power comparable in nature to South Africa or to the French in Algeria.

11 See Frédéric Abadie and Jean-Pierre Corcelette, *Valéry Giscard d'Estaing*, Balland, Paris, 1997, chapter VII.

12 Quoted in Frédéric Abadie and Jean-Pierre Corcelette, *Valéry Giscard d'Estaing*, Balland, Paris, 1997, p. 290. The reference is to the famous entry by Louis XVI in his diary for July 14, 1789: 'Rien'. He had been out hunting on the day of the fall of the Bastille, and had had no luck.

13 The matter is dealt with very fully on pp. 546–7 of *Le Quid des Présidents*, and on pp. 350–9 of Frédéric Abadie and Jean-Pierre Corcelette, who conclude their account by saying 'dans l'opinion publique, il ne restera qu'une seule trace: Giscard a reçu des diamants de Bokassa et ne les a

jamais rendus' (the public remembers only one thing: Giscard received diamonds from Bokassa, and never gave them back).

14 See his speech Act I, scene 4, reflecting on the effect which the drinking customs of the Danes have on their reputation for valour.

4 François Mitterrand: the rebellious brother

1 On February 4, 1998, *The Daily Telegraph* carried a long article, based on the cover story in the French political magazine *Marianne*, entitled 'All the presidents' women revealed at last'. If this article is to be believed, Mitterrand kept Anne Pigeot in a special suite of apartments in the Élysée Palace, and thus at the tax-payer's expense. Giscard d'Estaing, apparently, had an affair with the actress Claudia Cardinale, and had the habit of taking Sylvia Kristel, best known as the star of the film *Emmanuelle*, on trips abroad with him. However, the magazine *Elle* reported 83 per cent of French women said that the people had no right to know about the private life of the president.

2 *Le Monde*, September 2, 1994, in a review of Patrice Péan's *Une jeunesse française: François Mitterrand 1934–1947*, Plon, Paris, 1994.

3 See Appendix B in this volume

4 Routledge, London, 1994, second edn, 1997, p. 95.

5 Frémy – *Quid* gives crimes and indictable offences (*des délits*) rising from 2,890,000 in 1981 to 3.3 million in 1983. Although the rate of increase had fallen by 1984, this was a fact not immediately perceived by the average voter. As in the United States, the number of people of non-Caucasian origin in prison was much higher than their percentage in the general population. The high number of prisoners of North African origin was used by the National Front to support its policy of sending as many immigrants as possible back to their country of origin.

6 *Le Pouvoir et la vie*, vol. 2, Robert Laffont, Paris, 1991, p. 355.

7 *Le Quid des Présidents*, p. 601.

8 *Éditions du Journal officiel*, November 1997, pp. 121–8. See also, however, on pp. 128–33, *La Réponse du ministre de la fonction publique, de la réforme de l'État et de la décentralisation*.

9 See Jean-François Revel, *L'Absolutisme inefficace*, Plon, Paris, 1992, p. 102.

5 Jacques Chirac: the impulsive grandson

1 March, 1998.

2 See Nicholas Domenach and Maurice Szafran, *Le roman d'un Président*, Plon, Paris, 1997, p. 284.

3 Nicholas Domenach and Maurice Szafran, *Le roman d'un Président*, p. 84.

4 For details of the ranks in the French civil service see Philip Thody and Howard Evans, *Faux Amis and Key Words*, Athlone, London, 1985.

5 See Jean Charlot, *Pourquoi Jacques Chirac?*, Éditions de Fallois, Paris, 1995, p. 99.

6 Domenach and Szafran, *Le roman d'un Président*, 1997, p. 47.

7 Jean Charlot, *Pourquoi Jacques Chirac?*, p. 176.

8 See the description of her quoted by Frédéric Abadie and Jean-Pierre Corcelette on p. 292 of *Georges Pompidou, 1911–1974*. *Le désir et le destin*: 'une beauté, brune, dominatrice, que l'on imagine volontiers en bottes de cheval, la cravache à la main'. One sympathises with what Bertie Wooster would have felt when confronted with this mixture of Aunt Agatha *and* Aunt Dahlia. Frenchmen, however, tend to be less frightened of their womenfolk than the traditionally more timorous English male.

9 See *L'Événement du jeudi*, February 13, 1995. The official French for a bulldozer is 'un boutoir'. The attempt by the French to ban words of Anglo-American origin is studied in detail in my *Le Franglais. Forbidden English, Forbidden American. Law, Politics and Language in Contemporary France*, Athlone Press, London, 1995. Frank Richards' remark quoted in note 3 to chapter 3 applies in full.

10 Nicholas Domenach and Maurice Szafran, *Le roman d'un Président*, Plon, Paris, 1997, p. 185.

11 See Jean Charlot, *Pourquoi Jacques Chirac?* Éditions de Fallois, Paris, 1995, p. 47.

12 Stuart Hampshire, *Innocence and Experience*, Allen Lane, London, 1989, p. 163.

Annotated bibliography

Charles de Gaulle published more books than any other French president of the Fifth Republic. These include the three volumes of his *Mémoires de Guerre* (*L'Appel*, 1954; *L'Unité*, 1954 and *Le Salut*, 1954); and the two volumes of his *Mémoires d'espoir* (*Le Renouveau, 1958–1962*, 1970 and *L'Effort, 1962*, 1971), describing the events accompanying and following his return to power in 1958. *L'Effort* was left unfinished at his death. His most important pre-war books are *La Discorde chez l'ennemi*, 1924; *Vers l'armée de métier*, 1938; and *La France et son armée*, 1938. There are also five volumes of *Discours et Messages*, and nine volumes of *Lettres, Notes et Carnets*.

After 1945, all de Gaulle's works appeared under the imprint of the publishing house of Plon, a fact which created the irresistible temptation to make a pun about 'le soldat de plomb' (lead soldier). Jean Lacouture's definitive three volume study, *De Gaulle* (Éditions du Seuil, 1986) gives a complete list of de Gaulle's writings, as well as a full bibliography of everything published about him before 1986. He notes that de Gaulle's first book, *La Discorde chez l'ennemi*, was published in Paris in 1923 by the firm of Berger-Levrault, as were *Le Fil de l'épée* (1934) and *Vers l'armée de métier* (1934). This last, however, had first appeared in review form in January 1934 under the title 'Forgeons une armée de métier'.

There are naturally many other books on him, in English as well as in French. Don Cook's *Charles de Gaulle. A Biography* (Secker and Warburg, London, 1984); and Bernard Letwidge, *De Gaulle* (Weidenfeld and Nicolson, London, 1982) are excellent.

In addition to his 1944 edition of Racine's tragedy *Britannicus* in the Éditions Hachette, Paris, Georges Pompidou also published with Hachette, in 1955, in the Classiques Vauboudoule series, a selection of 'Pages choisies' from the novels of André Malraux (1901–76), who, after being one of the most distinguished fellow travellers of the 1930s, allied himself from 1944 onwards closely with de Gaulle. Pompidou's 1961 *Anthologie de la poésie française* was uncharitably described by the critic Joseph Barsalou as 'une anthologie de banquier: un porte-feuille de valeurs sûres' (a banker's anthology: a portfolio of blue chips).

Georges Pompidou's political writing includes a collection of essays, *Le Noeud gordien* (1974); and his *Entretiens et discours*, in two volumes, which appeared in 1975, the year immediately after his death. Appropriately enough, it was prefaced by Édouard Balladur, the only other prime minister of the Fifth Republic with practical experience of the business world. *Pour rétablir une vérité*, his account of the attempt to attack him by slandering his wife, was published by Flammarion, Paris, in 1982. As far as I know, there is no study of him in English, but there are two books in French: Éric Roussel, *Georges Pompidou. Le Président d'avant la crise*, Marabout, 1984; and Frédéric Abadie and Jean-Pierre Corcelette, *Georges Pompidou, 1911–1974. Le désir et le destin* (Balland, 1994).

Valéry Giscard d'Estaing's novel, *Le Passage*, was published in Paris by Robert Laffont in 1994. It describes how a successful lawyer meets a beautiful woman, Natalie, loses contact with her, searches endlessly for her until he finds and seduces her, only to lose her again. She is, according to Giscard d'Estaing, the symbol of modern youth, inaccessible because constantly in search of its own freedom. The hero, like the narrator, seems especially interested in how beautiful her legs are.

Giscard d'Estaing's political essays include the best-selling *La Démocratie Française*, 1976; *Le Pouvoir et la vie*, 1988, and *Deux Français sur trois*, 1984. The most recent study of him is Frédéric Abadie and Jean-Pierre Corcelette's *Valéry Giscard d'Estaing*, Balland, 1997. The best book on him is J. R. Frears, *France in the Giscard Presidency*, Allen and Unwin, London, 1981.

François Mitterrand was predictably prolix: *Au Frontières de l'Union française*, Julliard, Paris, 1953; *La Chine au défi*, Julliard, 1961; *Le coup d'état permanent*, Plon, 1964; *Technique de l'Économie française*, Fayard, Paris, 1968; *Ma part de vérité*, Plon, 1969; *Un socialisme du possible*, Fayard, Paris, 1971; *La Rose au poing*, Fayard, 1973; *La Paille et le Grain*, Fayard, 1975; *L'Abeille et l'Architecte*, Fayard, 1977. *Politique I* and *Politique II*, 1977 and 1981; *Ici et maintenant*, Fayard, 1980; *Réflexions sur la politique extérieure de la France*, Fayard, 1986;

and *Mémoires interrompus*, Fayard, 1996. Alistair Cole's excellent *François Mitterrand. A Study in Political Leadership*, Routledge, 1997 contains a very full bibliography.

Jacques Chirac has so far specialised in fairly short pamphlets: *Discours pour la France à l'heure du choix*, 1977; *La Lueur de l'espérance*, 1978; *Lettre à tous les Français*, 1995. As far as I know, there has as yet been no book on him in English, but the two main studies of him in French are mentioned in the notes: Nicholas Domenach and Maurice Szafran, *Le roman d'un Président*, Plon, 1997; and Jean Charlot, *Pourquoi Jacques Chirac?*, Éditions de Fallois, 1995. In 1998, Jean-Marie Colombani published his devastating *Le Résident à l'Élysée* (Stock), arguing how odd it was that the man whom he called, on p. 180. 'le Clausewitz des batailles électorales' should have become, by his mistake in dissolving the National Assembly in April 1997, 'celui qui a mis à terre la présidence gaullienne' (p. 300).

There are several excellent antidotes to my personalised approach to the history of the Fifth French Republic. One of the best is John Ardagh's *France Today*, first published by Penguin in 1982 and regularly updated. Serious students of the topics treated in my book will not neglect the excellent quarterly review published by the Association for the Study of Modern and Contemporary France.

Index

Page numbers in italics indicate main entry.

The image contains an index page from a book with entries in two columns.